Thirty Minutes to Raise the Dead

Thirty Minutes to Raise the Dead

HOW YOU CAN PREACH YOUR BEST SERMON YET— THIS SUNDAY

Bill Bennett

THOMAS NELSON PUBLISHERS
Nashville

Published in Nashville, Tennessee, by Thomas Nelson, Inc.,
and distributed in Canada by Lawson Falle, Ltd.,
Cambridge, Ontario.

Printed in the United States of America.

Unless otherwise noted, Scripture quotations are from the
NEW KING JAMES VERSION of the Bible. Copyright ©
1979, 1980, 1982, Thomas Nelson Publishers, Inc.

Scripture quotations noted NIV are from The Holy Bible:
NEW INTERNATIONAL VERSION. Copyright © 1978 by
the New York International Bible Society. Used by
permission of Zondervan Bible Publishers.

Scripture quotations noted TLB are from *The Living Bible*
(Wheaton, Illinois: Tyndale House Publishers, 1971) and are
used by permission.

Library of Congress Cataloging-in-Publication Data

Bennett, William, 1924–
    Thirty minutes to raise the dead / William Bennett.
        p.   cm.
    Includes bibliographical references.
    ISBN 0-8407-7676-4 (hard)
    1. Preaching.   I. Title.
BV4211.2.B44   1991
251—dc20   91–11304
                                                CIP

Printed in the United States of America

1 2 3 4 5 6 7 — 96 95 94 93 92 91

Bill Bennett is indeed the right person to give us a volume on expository preaching. His academic preparation is nothing short of outstanding. However, his primary accreditation for this work is the fact that he has done expository preaching with great effectiveness for more than thirty years. Bill Bennett is not writing simply as a theoretician. He is writing as a practitioner of effective expository preaching.

God, by His grace, enabled Bill Bennett to nurture one of the truly great evangelistic, missionary churches in America. The major thrust of this ministry in Fort Smith, Arkansas was the exposition of God's Word.

Bill Bennett is a scholar in the true sense of the word. He graduated with high honors, *Summa Cum Laude,* from one of America's most prestigious, academically respectable institutions of higher learning: Wake Forest University, where he earned the A.B. degree and was elected to Phi Beta Kappa. He also holds M.A. and Master of Divinity degrees from Duke University. He earned the Th.D. from New Orleans Baptist Theological Seminary where he also served as a teaching fellow.

This particular book is very practical and extremely warm. In reading through the manuscript, I was gratified to find a style that is clear and precise and extremely helpful. This same style is typical of this man of God's preaching.

This is not a book written from an armchair behind a mahogany desk. It is a plea from a heart pulsating with a desire to help and encourage fellow preachers and pastors, whom Bill Bennett calls "fellow strugglers in the way."

In my estimation, Bill Bennett practices what he preaches, and preaches what he practices. He is a soul-winner and believes strongly in the inerrancy of Holy Scripture.

CONTENTS

Conclusion: Ten Commandments

Notes

Acknowledgments

My homiletics professor at Duke University, Dr. James Clelland, defined preaching as an exercise in which a mere person is privileged to raise the dead in thirty minutes. I like this definition of preaching very much. Since preaching's primary objective is spiritual resurrection or the new birth, a preacher should be at the very best spiritually, physically, intellectually, emotionally, and professionally. I have prayerfully written this book as an encouragement for my fellow preachers to be maximum people for God.

I wish to express grateful appreciation to some very special people who have contributed greatly to my life and inspired me to write this book:

To my wife, Doris, who let me be alone with the Lord, with my books, and with the typewriter, long enough to grind out the manuscript;

To my ninety-eight-year-old mother who admonished me (and I obeyed) with these words, "When you preach, make it so simple that third graders can grasp it and perhaps the college students will understand";

To my father, the late Rev. Samuel L. Bennett, who without formal training was a powerful preacher of the gospel for more than a quarter of a century;

To Dr. Leo Eddleman, the erstwhile, erudite president of New Orleans Baptist Theological Seminary, who believed in me so deeply that I had to believe in myself to some extent;

To Dr. James Clelland, late professor of homiletics at Duke University, who laboriously tried to teach me the art of sermon preparation and delivery;

To Brother Jerry Bozeman, generous layman who provided a place of privacy and comfort overlooking beautiful Destin Beach, Florida, where I could write the manuscript;

To my pastoral interns, in whom I have endeavored to instill an incurable enthusiasm for expository preaching, both by example and teaching;

To all my churches, who have gladly received my preaching, expressed extravagant appreciation, and inspired me to become a better preacher: Calvary Baptist Church, Durham, North Carolina; Sixteenth Street Baptist Church, Greensboro, North Carolina; Clifton Baptist Church, Franklinton, Louisiana; Speedway Terrace Baptist Church, Memphis, Tennessee; First Baptist Church, Fort Smith, Arkansas; and Houston Northwest Baptist Church, Houston, Texas;

To that noble band of people across the world who have come to know Jesus through my preaching;

To the innumerable saints who have grown in grace and knowledge of our Lord Jesus Christ;

To that invisible army, now in heaven, who loved me, prayed for me, encouraged me, fed me, tolerated me, forgave me, and believed in me—in the best and the worst of times.

To all these—and many more—I express my everlasting thanks and indebtedness.

Soli Deo Gloria.

Introduction

A Personal Experience of the Anointing

I did not share the most sacred experience of my entire life for an entire year after it occurred. I hesitate to write of it even now. I do so only for the glory of our Lord Jesus Christ and for the encouragement it may afford to fellow strugglers along the way.

I was saved when I was nine years old. Accordingly, I was baptized by the Holy Spirit into the body of Christ at the same time (1 Cor. 12:13), at which time the Holy Spirit came into my heart to live forever (John 14:16). My compelling call to preach the gospel came at the age of twenty-five. I have never doubted for five minutes God's hand upon my life.

A year after graduating from seminary, I was called to pastor Sixteenth Street Baptist, a church of one thousand members in Greensboro, North Carolina. The church had been stagnant for years, but God began to stir the "dry bones" under my preaching. The church grew to be a leader in the association and state convention. I should have been happy and grateful, but I was neither. Preaching actually became a burden to my heart. I felt greatly relieved at the conclusion of my sermon on Sunday evenings, knowing I would not have to preach for another week.

I was dying on the inside, since I was ministering basically in the power of my flesh. I worked very hard but experienced little joy, and remaining in the ministry in such misery was torment. Rather than abandon my call, however, I sought an answer for my defeat. I believed that the infilling of the Holy Spirit was taught in the Bible. This conviction was strengthened by the testimonies of my father and mother, who were filled with the Holy Spirit. I began to search the Bible concerning the infilling of the Holy Spirit. Suddenly, there fell into my hand a book entitled *God Being My Helper,* by Ralph Herring, a respected Baptist pastor and Bible scholar, who related his experiences in being filled with the Holy Spirit. All these things, plus my great personal need, created within me an insatiable hunger for supernatural power in my life.

One day as I was walking the streets of Greensboro, I was suddenly overwhelmed with the presence of the Holy Spirit beside me. My experience was not in the realm of emotion but in the realm of revelation. I suddenly realized that the Holy Spirit was exactly who Jesus said he was, *the paracletos* (see John 14:16), and that he had come to stand by my side as my helper in every need. I immediately experienced a new joy, a new power, and a new freedom in preaching, praying, and evangelism. My ministry changed overnight. I found myself operating in the power of the Holy Spirit rather than the energy of my flesh.

This initial anointing set me on the road to a victorious ministry, for which I praise the Lord. I have experienced many fresh fillings since.

I do not want to be misunderstood. My encounter with the Holy Spirit did not become a cure for all my problems. I have walked in the valley and experienced some dark nights of the soul. I have preached when I felt little anointing. At times I felt I had failed. On many occasions I have ministered in "weakness, and fear and much trembling." Still, in the midst of all these things, I have always known a source of power greater than my weaknesses. I have discovered that "He who is in you is greater than he who is in the world" (1 John 4:4), that "I can do all things through Christ who strengthens me" (Phil. 4:13), and that the Lord's "strength is made perfect in weakness" (2 Cor. 12:9).

No other believer should seek my experience, but I would plead that every believer seek the experience that God has for him with the Holy Spirit. In particular, every preacher should seek a fresh anointing every time he stands to proclaim the Word of the living God.

PART ONE

The Power to Raise the Dead

CHAPTER 1

The Power of Preaching

Truth is conveyed through the ordinances of baptism and the Lord's Supper when they are rightly observed. Truth can be put to music. Truth can be written and read. Truth can be shared through counseling, exhortation, and dialogue. But none of these media can ever replace preaching. Preaching is central to Christianity. When we substitute any conveyor of truth for preaching the Truth, the church is weakened and God's people become spiritually anemic. In fact, God has ordained preaching as His chief means of confronting fallen humanity with His saving message.

Survey the great churches of history and the present, and you will find great preaching of the Word of God. Sometimes a work of God may appear to be grounded in Christian education, counseling, or music. When the religious dust settles, however, the primary ingredient for building a great work of God is the preaching of God's Word. This is not to imply that other ministries have no place in the church. But preaching should be the basis; all other ministries should be corollaries.

Twenty-five years ago, the pastor of a prominent Southern Baptist church said to me, "The way to build a great church is through the training of children in Sunday school." But at his retirement he acknowledged he had not built a great church because he had not emphasized preaching. The apostle Paul declares the importance of preaching in 1 Corinthians 1:21: "It pleased God through the foolishness of the message preached to save those who believe."

The Indispensable Place of Preaching

The twentieth century has produced some great authorities on preaching. Listen to these four men on the primacy of preaching in the Christian enterprise.

Andrew W. Blackwood declared:

Preaching should rank as the noblest work on earth. The man called of God to preach the gospel ought to stand out as the most important man in the community, and all he

does for Christ and the church should head up
in his preaching.[1]

W. E. Sangster acclaimed:

Called to preach. . . . Commissioned of God to
teach the Word! A herald of the great King! A
witness of the eternal gospel! Could any work
be more high and holy? To this supreme task
God sent his only begotten Son. In all the
frustration and confusion of the times, is it
possible to imagine a work comparable in
importance with that of proclaiming the will of
God to wayward men?[2]

Martyn Loyd-Jones asserted:

To me the work of preaching is the highest and
the greatest and the most glorious calling to
which anyone can ever be called. If you want
something in addition to that, I would say
without hesitation that the most urgent need in
the Christian church today is true preaching.
There is nothing like it. It is the greatest work
in the world, the most thrilling, the most
exciting, the most rewarding, and the most
wonderful.[3]

John R. Stott said:

Preaching is indispensable to Christianity. For
Christianity is, in its very essence, a religion of
the Word of God. First, God spoke through the
prophets . . . instructing them to convey his
message to his people either by speech or by

writing or both. Next . . . he spoke in his Son,
his Words . . . made flesh, and in his Word . . .
spoken directly or through his apostles.
Thirdly, he speaks through his Spirit who
himself bears witness to Christ and to
Scripture. . . . This Trinitarian statement of a
speaking Father, Son, and Holy Spirit, and so
of a Word of God that is scriptural, incarnate,
and contemporary, is fundamental to the
Christian religion. And it is God's speech
which makes our speech necessary. We must
speak what he has spoken. Hence the
paramount obligation to preach.[4]

The Bible, history, students of preaching,
and our own experiences attest to the importance of preaching for the Christian faith. I
have pastored churches for forty years, serv-
ing congregations ranging from eighty-five
to eight thousand members. In all of these
churches I witnessed dynamic spiritual re-
newal, primarily through the proclamation of
the inscripturated Word of God. To young
preachers across America I say, "Give your
mornings to God and to the study of the Word
of God." I know of no preacher who has followed this pattern who has not succeeded.

What is preaching? Phillips Brooks' classic
definition would be hard to improve. In his famous Beecher Lectures at Yale University, he
said that preaching is "the bringing of truth
through personality" or "the communication
of truth by man to men."[5]

The history of Israel and the Christian church witness to the power of "truth through personality." The Old Testament prophets stood head and shoulders above other men. The dominant figures of the New Testament were preachers, beginning with Jesus, and followed by Peter, Paul, the author of Hebrews, and Apollos. The New Testament abounds in preaching as reported through the biblical writers.[6]

A History of Christian Preaching

The history of the early church demonstrates the powerful influence of preaching, as well. Whenever the tides of spiritual power stood at their zenith, preaching stood first in the work of Christian leaders.

Students have noted eight historical periods in the development of Christian preaching. I believe the chief factors producing each stage have been the varying attitudes toward the authority of the Bible and of the place of preaching in the church. From an historical perspective, the great eras of preaching have also been the great periods of Christian growth.

The Ancient or Patristic Period (A.D. 70–430)

Peter, Paul, Chrysostom, Augustine, and Ambrose were preachers who had an impact on history by speaking God's Word. Flexibility and informality characterized preaching during these early years. Many preachers spoke only as the "Holy Spirit gave them utterance."

The Middle or Dark Ages (A.D. 430–1095)

These years saw the power of the pulpit all but destroyed as sacerdotalism settled over the civilized world. Only priests had power to mediate between God and man; expounding the Scriptures to the people was viewed as unnecessary and even dangerous. "Where there is no revelation, the people cast off restraint" (Prov. 29:18). Such was the case during this time when there was little preaching of the pure Word of God. Some scholars believe that the great dearth of biblical preaching accounts primarily for the "Dark Ages."

The Scholastic Age (A.D. 1095–1361)

This period ushered in a new era of learning which enhanced preaching to some extent. This was the age of Bernard of Clairvaux, Francis of Assisi, and Dominic, all regarded as superlative preachers.

The Reformation Age (A.D. 1361–1572)

The Reformation brought a genuine revival in preaching. The Bible was the supreme authority, the believer was his own priest, and the sermon was in the language of the people. Indeed, the pulpit was raised above the altar and became the central focus in the architecture of the churches. Probably if anyone had asked Martin Luther what he regarded as his primary call, he would have said preaching. So would John Calvin, John Knox. Ulrich Zwingli, Balthasar Hubmaier, and other leaders of the Reformation. Not only did preaching play a major role in the revival of the Church, but also in the revival of civilization.

The Seventeenth Century (A.D. 1572–1700)

Preaching declined throughout most of the Christian world, except in England and France.

The Eighteenth Century (A.D. 1701–1800)

The eighteenth century was marked by the powerful preaching of John Wesley, George Whitefield, Jonathan Edwards, and others on the American scene. Their thunderous sermons revolutionized English society and helped bring spiritual awakening to the American colonies. The historian, William Edward Leeky, concluded that this revival saved England from the moral destruction that befell France during the same century.

The Nineteenth Century (A.D. 1801–1900)

The nineteenth century produced an array of mighty preachers and again the church flourished. It is not accidental that this century saw the expansion of Christianity across the earth. Great personalities dominated the preaching of this century, such as Charles H. Spurgeon, Dwight L. Moody, F. B. Meyer, Alexander Maclaren, and John H. Broadus. These men preached the Word of God with clarity, vividness, and power. This century has been compared to the first century of Peter and Paul, and to the fourth century of Chrysostom and Augustine.

The Twentieth Century

The first seventy years of this century witnessed a decline in preaching, and the church suffered great loss. The role of the pastor changed during this period. Professors H. G. Brown, H. Gordon Clinard, and James Northcutt observed:

> The unparalleled growth of churches and the demands of a materialistic society have forced ministers to relegate study and sermon preparation to a secondary role, while the role of administrator, pastor, organizer, counselor, and teacher superseded that of preacher.[7]

But in many circles a revival of preaching is now taking place.

Whenever Christianity has made great progress, great preaching has led the way. According to Brown, Clinard, and Northcutt:

> God ordained preaching to proclaim his message to all mankind. When preachers have failed to understand God's method and message, God's kingdom has been hindered. When men heard God's call, understood their task, and faithfully delivered his message, the kingdom has moved forward for his glory.[8]

Let us pray that preaching may be restored to its central place, its apostolic primacy, and to the indispensable role that our Sovereign God has assigned to it.

The Legacy of Expository Preaching

Preaching is a rather general term. So if you ask me what kind of preaching moves the church forward, I would identify expository, or biblical, preaching.

Expository preaching dates at least as far back as Ezra, the scribe. Robert Dabney says, "It was under Ezra that preaching assumed ... more nearly its modern place as a constant part of worship, and also its modern character, as an exposition of the written Scriptures."[9]

Nehemiah 8:1–8 reveals the expository approach of Ezra:

> Now all the people gathered together as one
> man in the open square that was in front of the
> Water Gate; and they told Ezra the scribe to
> bring the Book of the Law of Moses, which
> the LORD had commanded Israel. So Ezra
> the priest brought the Law before the
> congregation, of men and women and all who
> could hear with understanding, on the first day
> of the seventh month. Then he read from it . . .
> in front of the Water Gate from morning until
> midday, before the men and women and those
> who could understand; and the ears of all the
> people were attentive to the Book of the Law.
> So Ezra the scribe stood on a platform of wood
> which they had made for the purpose. . . . And
> Ezra opened the book in the sight of all the
> people, for he was standing above all the
> people; and when he opened it, all the people
> stood up. And Ezra blessed the LORD, the great
> God. . . . So they read distinctly from the book,
> in the Law of God; and they gave the sense,
> and helped them to understand the reading.

Nehemiah 8:8 (NIV) reads, "They read from
the Book of the Law of God, making it clear
and giving the meaning so that the people
could understand what was being read."

This account accurately describes the work
of the expositor. The Scriptures were read in
the hearing of the people; an interpretation

was given so the people could understand their meaning; and, in all probability, application was made to their lives. At least from this time, the Holy Scriptures were read and then expounded as a regular exercise in the services of the synagogues.[10]

In Nehemiah 9:3 we read that "they stood up in their place and read from the Book of the Law of the LORD their God for one-fourth of the day." The remainder of the chapter is an historical exposition of God's mercy and goodness to Israel, which are typical illustrations of Old Testament preaching. In the centuries prior to the advent of Christ and although corrupted by tradition and spiritual blindness, this method was still in vogue when Jesus began his public ministry.[11]

The great preacher and teacher, Jesus Christ was superior to all expositors. Though his doctrine was clearly different from then prevalent theology, he adopted the time-honored method of reading and expounding the Holy Scriptures. Publicly and privately, Jesus opened the Scriptures to the understanding of the people. Mark 1:21-22 says, "And they went into Capernaum, and immediately on the Sabbath He entered the synagogue and taught. And they were astonished at His teaching, for He taught them as one having authority, and not as the scribes." Mark 2:1-2 reads, "And again He entered Capernaum after some days, and it was heard that He was in the house. Immediately many gathered together, so that there was no longer room to receive them. . . . And He preached the word to them." Again, Mark 4:34 asserts that when they were alone, he expounded all things to his disciples.

Perhaps the most notable examples of public exposition on the part of Jesus are found in Luke's gospel. Jesus came to Nazareth where he had been brought up,

> And as His custom was, He went into the synagogue on the Sabbath day, and stood up for to read. And He was handed the book of the prophet Isaiah. And when He had opened the book, He found the place where it was written:
>
> *The Spirit of the LORD is upon Me,*
> *Because He has anointed Me to preach the*
>   *gospel to the poor.*
> *He has sent Me to heal the brokenhearted,*
> *To preach deliverance to the captives*
> *And recovery of sight to the blind,*
> *To set at liberty those who are oppressed,*
> *To preach the acceptable year of the Lord.*
>
> Then He closed the book, and gave it back to the attendant and sat down. And the eyes of all who were in the synagogue were fixed on Him. And He began to say to them, "Today this Scripture is fulfilled in your hearing." So all bore witness to Him, and marveled at the gracious words which proceeded out of His mouth (Luke 4:16–22).

Please note that it was the custom of Jesus to read the Scriptures publicly in the synagogues on the Sabbath. Though Jesus actually read only two verses from Isaiah, he probably gave an extended exposition of these verses in their context. The record declares that all the people in the synagogue were "filled with wrath" and tried to murder Jesus by pushing him over the cliff (see Luke 4:28–30). The mere reading of the Scripture, without exposition and application, would scarcely have produced such a violent uproar.

Another example of his exposition took place on the Emmaus Road.

Then He said to them, "O foolish ones, and slow of heart to believe in all that the prophets have spoken! Ought not the Christ to have suffered these things and to enter into His glory?" And beginning at Moses and all the Prophets, He expounded to them in all the Scriptures the things concerning Himself. . . . And they said to one another, "Did not our heart burn within us while He talked with us on the road, and while He opened the Scriptures to us?" So they rose up that very hour and returned to Jerusalem, and found the eleven and those who were with them gathered together, saying, "The Lord is risen indeed. . . ." And they told about the things that had happened on the road, and how He was known to them in the breaking of bread (Luke 24:25–27, 32–35).

Jesus must have talked quite a long time as he expounded "the things concerning himself" throughout the Hebrew Bible. This expository opening of the Scriptures sent these discouraged, hopeless disciples back to the city of Jerusalem, on the same night, with a glowing testimony of a restored and renewed faith. Indeed, they described their experience as divine heartburn as they listened to Jesus: "Did not our heart burn within us while He talked with us on the road, and while He opened the Scriptures to us?" (Luke 24:32).

The first gospel message by Peter on the Day of Pentecost is an exposition of passages from Joel and the Psalms (see Acts 2). Stephen's address in Acts 7 is an expository dissertation based upon Genesis, Exodus, and a brief summary of the Babylonian captivity. Philip followed the same procedure with the Ethiopian eunuch by expounding Isaiah 53 and pointing out that the passage spoke about Jesus Christ (see Acts 8:26–35). The eunuch received Jesus as his personal Savior and Lord on the basis of Philip's preaching, and Philip baptized him upon his clear confession of faith.

The apostle Paul was second only to Jesus as an expositor. When Paul and his team had passed through Amphipolis and Apollonia, "they came to Thessalonica, where there was a synagogue of the Jews. And Paul, as his custom was, went in to them, and for three Sabbaths reasoned with them from the Scriptures, explaining . . . that the Christ had to suffer and rise again from the dead, and saying, 'This Jesus whom I preach to you is the Christ'" (Acts 17:1-3).

The last glimpse of Paul in Acts shows him expounding the Scriptures. "And when they had appointed him a day, many came to him at his lodging, to whom he explained and solemnly testified of the kingdom of God, persuading them concerning Jesus from both the Law of Moses and the Prophets, from morning till evening" (Acts 28:23). Paul never undertook to establish the truth about the living Christ from logic, philosophy, or personal experiences. Rather, he simply persuaded the people that Jesus of Nazareth was the Christ, the Messiah, with logical evidence from expounding the Old Testament Scriptures. Paul evidently continued to expound the Scriptures until the day of his death. Just prior to his execution, he requested Timothy to bring him "the books" and "the parchments" (see 2 Tim. 4:13). "Books" were probably rabbinic commentaries written on papyrus. The "parchments" (vellum) were more likely Old Testament manuscripts which Paul especially desired.

Further evidence that Paul greatly esteemed the expository method is revealed in his counsel to young Timothy to give himself to exposition. In 1 Timothy 4:13 he wrote, "Till I come, give attention to reading, to exhortation, to doctrine." Then Paul says to Timothy:

> All Scripture is God-breathed [NIV], and is profitable for doctrine, for reproof, for correction, for instruction in righteousness, that the man of God may be complete, thoroughly equipped for every good work. I charge you therefore before God and the Lord Jesus Christ, who will judge the living and the dead at His appearing and His kingdom: Preach the word! Be ready in season and out of season. Convince, rebuke, exhort, with all longsuffering and teaching. For the time will come when they will not endure sound doctrine, but according to their own desires, because they have itching ears, they will heap up for themselves teachers; and they will turn their ears away from the truth, and be turned aside to fables. But you be watchful in all things, endure afflictions, do the work of an evangelist, fulfill your ministry (2 Tim. 3:16—4:5).

Taken in light of the context, the command, "Preach the Word," could mean nothing less than what we call expository preaching.[12]

Douglas White contends that the expositional method of preaching was used almost exclusively in apostolic times. The two renowned preachers of the early church, Augustine and Chrysostom, left volumes of expository messages on the books of Genesis,

Psalms, Matthew, John, and the epistles of Paul. There can be little doubt, writes White, that expository preaching was predominant for at least twelve centuries:

> Just as the decline of the spiritual life of the Church was gradual, so, doubtless, was the departure from the apostolic method of preaching. As the distinction between church and state diminished and as ritualism, tradition, and superstition increased (bringing about the papal system which remains today), so the distinction between the church and the world decreased. As the Bible ceased to be recognized as the final authority in all matters pertaining to religion, and more and more authority was claimed by the Pope and ecclesiasticism, the apostolic polity of the church waned. Instead of following . . . the biblical order of preaching, and the precedent set by the apostles, ministers began to adopt methods of their own devising, which would be designed for acceptance by the congregations to which they ministered, but without the authority and power of the Holy Spirit.[13]

White concludes that this "could not have happened overnight, but it is highly significant that the wholesale departure from expository . . . preaching was followed by the spiritual eclipse, known as the Dark Ages."[14] J. W. Alexander added, "When the light of divine truth began to emerge from its long eclipse at the Reformation, there were few things more remarkable than the universal return of evangelicals to expository preaching."[15] Martin Luther's exposition redeemed Christendom from the Dark Ages and instituted the Reformation. Again, Douglas White observes:

> Nevertheless, the prevalence of expositional preaching was comparatively short-lived. History has been repeating itself. The process has been slow . . . but the departure has been just about as widespread as before. Along with it has come a multitude of cults, and other satanic, subversive influences. The departure has been far more noticeable during the last two centuries. . . . This fact, undoubtedly, accounts for the spiritually anemic condition of the church universally; the widespread apostasy in territories where the gospel has been preached . . . and the tremendous inroads of cults and false religions in all parts of the world.[16]

Surely the modern world has suffered greatly from a general lack of expository preaching. But, as we shall see, there is an upsurge of expository preaching in some circles today. All preachers should heed the words of the great advocate of expository preaching, Dr. H. Jeffs:

The Bible is the preacher's book and the preacher's glory. Bible exposition is the preacher's main business. If he cannot or will not expound the Bible, what right has he in any pulpit? He is a cumberer of the ground that might be occupied by a fruit bearing and soul nourishing tree. If he does not expound the Bible, what else is there for him to do? He may deliver addresses out of his head on any subject that occurs to him, and he may do it well, but why do it in the pulpit? It is his own gospel, or has he a gospel that might just as well be preached without the Bible as with it? He is presumably a preacher of a Christian church, but there would be no Christian church today had there been no Bible. So long as there remains the triple tragedy of sin, suffering, and death, so long will the Bible speak to the heart of man. And, humanity that has once known the Bible will turn away (after the novelty has worn off) from every flashy substitute of the Bible that our modern Athenians push as the latest things in the spiritual market.[17]

CHAPTER 2

But What Happened to the Power?

While the eternal God has ordained that his saving message be propagated by preaching, humankind has not regarded preaching with such favor. Some go so far as to say that preaching is a dying art, an outmoded form of communication, an echo from an abandoned past.[1]

What happened to the power of preaching to affect men's lives? We can identify various reasons for the contemporary disenchantment with preaching. Let's consider some of these, beginning with the most significant.

The Rejection of the Authority of the Word of God

For many biblical criticism has undermined biblical authority. First confined to theological seminaries, this problem soon spread to the pulpits; now it has filtered down to the pews. Even some circles in the Bible Belt have felt the blight of higher criticism. The literature published by most major denominations reflects a view of the Scriptures formed by historical-critical methodology.

In the past, cardinal doctrines of the Christian faith were denied. But in our day the attack has shifted to the nature and authority of the Bible itself. Many leading seminaries in America and throughout the world teach that the Bible only *contains* the Word of God, that the Bible *is not* the Word of God in its entirety. This view holds that the Bible is reliable only when it speaks on religious matters, but it errs in matters of history, geography, and science. Miracles are denied or explained away by many; literal history is interpreted as figurative or parabolic. Consequently, many graduates leave their studies with a mutilated Bible, one that cannot be totally trusted or preached. When I asserted at a prestigious eastern seminary that Luther and Calvin believed in an infallible Bible and that they reflected the historic position of the Church, my position was belittled. Though I proved my point by quoting the testimonies of Luther and Calvin, I did not convince the professor or all of the students.

Without total confidence in the Bible, strong preaching is impossible. John Stott believes that there is no possibility of the recovery of preaching without a prior recovery of the conviction of a totally reliable Bible. G. Campbell Morgan, the gifted expositor who once himself questioned the Bible, spoke a very strong word on the absolute necessity to proclaim the Word with absolute certainty:

> Preaching is not the proclamation of a theory, or the discussion of doubt. A man has a perfect right to proclaim a theory of any sort, or to discuss his doubts. But that is not preaching. "Give me the benefit of your convictions, if you have any. Keep your doubts to yourself, I have enough of my own," said Johann Wolfgang Von Goethe. We are never preaching when we are hazarding speculations. . . . We are bound to speculate sometimes. I sometimes say, "I am speculating; stop taking notes." Speculation is not preaching. Preaching is the proclamation of the Word, the truth as the truth has been revealed.[2]

Martin Loyd-Jones, described by some as the "last of the preachers," says there is no doubt that the modern reaction against preaching is primarily due to "the loss of belief in the authority of the Scriptures and a diminution in the belief of the Truth."[3]

The Revolt Against Authority

Rebellion is not new; it reaches back to the fall of man. Paul declared that the carnal mind

38

is unable to submit to God's authority (see Rom. 8:7). What seems new today, however, is the worldwide revolt against authority and the philosophical arguments with which it is supported. There can be no doubt that the twentieth century—and especially the latter half—has been caught up in a global revolution against all accepted authorities: the Bible, the church, the family, the Pope, God, the school, the university, and, of course, preaching. Teenagers are notorious for saying to their parents, "Don't preach to me." And this is also what much of the world is saying to preachers.

We may be living in the day which Jesus predicted, "Because lawlessness will abound, the love of many will grow cold" (Matt. 24:12). The late Vance Havner described our age as one of "abounding lawlessness and abating love." This spirit of lawlessness will increase until Jesus comes again. In such a rebellious age authoritative preaching will be held in contempt by those in revolt.

The Rise of Relativism

Closely related to the loss in biblical authority has been the increasing acceptance of relativism—the widespread view that there are no absolutes. Secular humanism, a major American force that has been declared a "religion" by our Supreme Court, blatantly asserts that there is no absolute truth. With such a conviction, there is no place for the preacher who says, "Thus saith the Lord." Realizing this fact, too many fearful preachers have substituted a "Thus saith Dr. Sounding Brass" or "Thus saith Professor Dry as Dust" as their authority.

Apply relativism to doctrine and ethics, and absolutes are abandoned. Darwinism convinced many that religion is an evolutionary phase in man's history. Marx said that religion is only a sociological phenomenon. Freud insisted that religion is a neurosis. The comparative study of religions attempted to downgrade Christianity to just another religion. Existentialism insists that nothing matters but the experience of the moment. The denials of radical theology teach that there is no loving, personal God and that Jesus is not God.

Adherence to such views has contributed to a loss of nerve among preachers. Some frankly confess that they see their function as sharing their own doubts with their congregation.[4] Such is the frightful fruitage of relativism. In such an atmosphere the odds are stacked against the preacher of the Word of God.

Television's Effect on People's Listening Ability

Americans spend an average of 23.3 hours per week viewing television. Does this kind of activity have an effect on people's ability to *listen* to sermons? Dr. John R. Stott has made a careful study of this phenomenon and reached some helpful conclusions which indicate that television makes it harder for preachers to hold a congregation's attention and secure an appropriate response.

First, a steady diet of television tends to make people physically lazy, offering them home entertainment at the turn of a knob. Why not relax in a comfortable armchair and worship before the screen? Why bother to turn out for church? Second, television also tends to make people intellectually critical. People flop before the box to be entertained, not to think. So the disease of "spectatoritis" is widespread in society today. Third, the constant viewing of television leads to emotional insensitivity. We have viewed so much pain and tragedy that we have become hardened to human need. Fourth, too much viewing can cause psychological confusion. We are bombarded with so many conflicting reports that we find ourselves bewildered as to the truth. Fifth, the vivid immorality and raw crime portrayed make viewers morally disordered. And sixth, I have also observed that television can be a substitute for the local church, undermining its authority and that of the pastor.

In the light of the profound impact of TV upon the human psyche, we can no longer assume that people either want to listen to sermons or have the ability to do so. Observes Stott,

> When they are accustomed to the swiftly moving images of the screen, how can we expect them to give their attention to one person talking, with no frills, no light relief and nothing else to look at? Is it not beyond them? In consequence, when the sermon begins, they switch off.[5]

Stott may have overstated it, but there can be no doubt that a steady diet of television is a major hindrance to preaching in our day.

Problems in the Pulpit

The preacher himself is often a major hindrance to the acceptance of preaching. Much preaching is void of biblical content, poorly prepared, and lacking the anointing of the Holy Spirit. The result is that the people are not fed the living Word of God. John Milton said, "The hungry sheep look up and are not fed." And hungry sheep will not return forever to the place where there is no food.

Reaction Against Showmanship in the Pulpit

The nineteenth century witnessed the emergence of the so-called "pulpiteers." These men, though godly, were nevertheless showmen who played heavily on the emotions, often controlling and mesmerizing their hearers. This tendency has continued into the twentieth century in some circles. While some people flock to hear such men, others have "turned them off."[6] The recent abuses and scandals of televangelists will only increase this reaction.

The Element of Worship

In many churches preaching has been relegated to a secondary place. In its place ritual, music, responsive reading, drama, and videos have been substituted. These substitutes are justified on the ground that they are enriching worship, but often in the process, preaching has suffered.

Martin Loyd-Jones believed also that celebrity testimonies, many solo presentations, and films are forms of entertainment. "This is what the church has been turning to as she has turned her back on preaching."[7] I too have noted this tendency with considerable concern as I have preached across the country. One gets the impression that preaching is not the most important thing in a worship service. Rather singing, testimonies, and even announcements get center stage. When a preacher is given only fifteen or twenty minutes to deliver his sermon, what does that say about the place of preaching?

Substitutes

"As preaching goes down," observed Martin Loyd-Jones, "personal counseling goes up."[8] With the increase in personal problems, counseling has become paramount in many churches. There is certainly a place for biblically oriented counseling, but it should never be substituted for preaching. In fact, good preaching is counseling *en masse,* making much personal counseling unnecessary.

A growing number of people substitute listening to tapes for hearing live sermons. Why go to the trouble of attending church when you can listen to a sermon while driving to work? This is not to deny the valid motives of many who faithfully attend their church and hear sermons and also listen to tapes as enrichment to their spiritual food.

The climate of our times is not conducive for the preacher to speak and for the people to listen. As Stott cleverly summed up the situation, "A dumb preacher with a deaf congregation presents a fearsome barrier of communication."[9] Still, the Holy Spirit is breaking down this barrier. The best defense against the attack on preaching is a counterattack. Therefore, I propose the unleashing of an unprecedented wave of expository preaching across the earth, and this book is dedicated to this end.

PART TWO

Reaching the Dead and Buried

CHAPTER 3

The Nature of Expository Preaching

Expository preaching is the preaching of the Bible and communicating the message of God. Expository preaching does not depend upon the length of the biblical passage, but rather the way the passage is handled. Dr. John Stott, contemporary authority on preaching, says in this connection, "The text in question could be a verse, or a sentence, or even a single word. It could equally be a paragraph, chapter, or whole book. The size of the text is immaterial so long as it is biblical. What matters is what we do with it."[1]

Expository preaching is not, therefore, restricted to the exposition of successive passages in books of the Bible. Faithful exposition of books of the Bible, or of a text in its context, qualifies as expository preaching. Though some topics may be handled expositionally, most textual and topical sermons are not expository.

Definition of Expository Preaching

As Faris Whitesell has observed, an expository sermon is one based on a Bible passage, usually (but not always) longer than a verse or two. The theme and major divisions come from the passage, the whole sermon being an honest attempt to unfold the true grammatical, historical, and contextual meaning of the passage, making it relevant today by proper organization, argument, illustration, and appeal.[2]

For the sake of absolute clarity, this definition can be broken down into these seven ingredients. Expository preaching must:

1. be based on a passage in the Bible, either short or long;
2. focus on the primary meaning of the passage;
3. relate the passage's meaning to its context;
4. search for the timeless truths in the text;
5. organize these truths around one central theme;
6. employ the rhetorical devices of

explanation, argumentation, illustration, and application to apply the truth of the passage to the hearer; and
7. seek to persuade the hearers to obey the truth presented.[3]

Expositor Craig Skinner offers this definition:

Expository preaching is the art of proclaiming selected, significant, timeless truth from a Bible passage which begins with faithful exegesis, continues with a full understanding and analysis of the context of that passage, is shaped by a constant reference to the truth contained in that passage, and presents this material as a relevant message of spiritual power, clearly linked to the needs of hearers today.[4]

Haddon Robinson, professor of homiletics for nineteen years at Dallas Theological Seminary and now president at Denver Seminary, defines expository preaching much like the above, but with an added dimension. "Expository preaching," he writes, "is the communication of a biblical concept derived from and transmitted through a historical, grammatical study of a passage in its context which the Holy Spirit first applies to the personality and experience of the preacher and then through him to the hearer."[5]

Categories of Expository Preaching

Since preaching is "truth through personality" and expository preaching varies in its approach, no two expository preachers expound the Scriptures alike. All seek to unfold, illuminate, illustrate, and apply the truth of the Scriptures, although each goes about it in a different way.

Faris D. Whitesell, who is a major modern advocate of expository preaching, has studied the great expository preachers of history and has classified expository preaching into fifteen categories as exemplified in the preaching of specific men. These various approaches to expository preaching need to be identified, not because all represent good expository preaching, but to illustrate the wide variety possible in the exposition of the Word of God. The fifteen types and at least one good, flesh-and-blood example from history are as follows:[6]

1. The *disciplined approach*—Alexander Maclaren shut himself in his study every day of the week and devoted many exacting hours to the preparation of each sermon.

2. The *contextual principle*—G. Campbell Morgan closely related every text to its

total context, often developing fresh interpretations of familiar passages.

3. The *balanced approach*—Frederick W. Robertson excelled in preaching sermons with two main points, thus laying stress on the principle of balance.

4. The *imaginative approach*—Joseph Parker's material is original, colorful, and vivid.

5. The *pivot text method*—F. B. Meyer specialized in selecting a pivotal text and developing his exposition around it.

6. The *inverted pyramid approach*—Donald G. Barnhouse insisted that "the only way to understand any given passage in the Word of God is to take the whole Bible and place the point of it, like an inverted pyramid on that passage, so that the weight of the entire Word rests upon a single verse, or indeed a single word."[7]

7. The *single subject method*—Roy Laurin chose the idea of "Life" as the key to open several books of the Bible.

8. The *author-centered approach*—Paul S. Rees expounds Philippians as a self-portrait of its author, Paul.

9. The *background approach*—George Adam Smith and Harris E. Kirk made effective use of background materials in their exposition.

10. The *running-commentary approach*—

H. A. Ironside made verse-to-verse comments on most of the books of the Bible. This method was used by Chrysostom, Luther, Calvin, and Zwingli. I used this method for ten years in building a large Bible class at First Baptist Church, Ft. Smith, Arkansas.

11. The *lesson method*—William M. Taylor and J. C. Ryle stressed and applied the practical lessons in the Scriptures.

12. The *analytical method*—Griffith Thomas excelled in analyzing a passage and putting it in structural outlines.

13. The *exegetical approach*—A. T. Robertson and William Barclay were masters of Greek and could expound the meaning of Greek words more easily than the average preacher can do it in English.

14. The *stylistic emphasis*—John Henry Jowett's hobby was the study of words, and he would write, rewrite, correct, and rewrite to perfect his style.

15. The *evangelistic method*—William Riley and George Truett turned the Scriptures to evangelistic ends.

The Holy Spirit uses the personalities and abilities of men in expounding the Scriptures in different ways, even as he used different personalities in writing the Holy Scriptures (see 2 Pet. 1:20–21). No clones exist in expository preaching. Expository preaching, while always biblical and always expounding a co-herent core of truth, varies in forms. I have heard quite a few expository sermons on John 3 in which each preacher expounded the time-less truth of the new birth; however, each ser-mon was refreshingly different. In fact, I have expounded John 3 quite a few times, and each exposition has been quite different.

Methods of Expository Preaching

Merrill F. Unger, widely recognized among evangelical scholars, sees three main ap-proaches to expository preaching; namely, the running-commentary method, the Bible-reading method, and the purely expositional method.[8]

We must not, however, impose too narrow a definition upon expository preaching. While undoubtedly an important and the most obvi-ous method, expository preaching is more than a series of sermons expounding some book or books of the Bible. Unger is correct when he contends that if we narrowly define expository preaching, we may cause preach-ers to become discouraged with this method, find it monotonous, and abandon it altogether.[9]

Topical Presentation

The purpose of any method of preaching must be to present the Truth fully and clearly for the purpose of securing a verdict. Often the best way to expound the Truth of the Scriptures is under a topic, such as a biblical doctrine. The particular doctrine chosen becomes the topic. Ordinarily a single scriptural text presents only one aspect of the doctrine, and so a number of key passages must be selected and expounded in their contexts to give a comprehensive view.[10]

W. H. Griffith Thomas treated the topic of justification expositorily, explaining "the doctrine of justification in proper focus upon the full Scriptural revelation on the subject."[11] In this sermon, Thomas raised four fundamental questions about justification and answered them fully from the Scriptures: 1.) What is the meaning of justification? 2.) What is the basis of justification? 3.) What is the method of justification? and 4.) What is the value of justification?

Some may contend that Thomas would have had a better sermon if he had expounded Romans 5:1–5, the classic text on justification. This may be true, but, in his approach, Thomas covered several important facets about justification not answered in the fifth chapter of Romans.[12]

Biographical Sermons

Biographical characters also lend themselves to the expository method. Many Bible characters yield themselves to admirable treatment when their careers are interpreted around some central, unifying truth from Scripture. A. B. Simpson, a gifted expositor, excelled in the biographical sermon, and a somewhat more recent master of the biographical sermon was Clarence McCartney. Simpson's treatment of Isaac is a good example of the expository biographical sermon. He entitled his sermon "Isaac: The Patience of Faith" and divided it into four parts: 1.) Painful Trials as a Child, 2.) Severe Tests as a Youth, 3.) Faithful Choices as a Young Man, and 4.) Faith and Patience toward the Trials of Life.[13]

Textual Expository Messages

The textual sermon can also be expositional in method if the text is faithfully expounded, set in its contextual background, and given proper illustrations and application. Whenever the preacher applies the expository method to his text, he will be preaching an expository sermon. Merrill F. Unger observed in this connection, "The only difference from a purely expository message, as commonly conceived, will be the shorter length of the passage elucidated."[14]

Charles Haddon Spurgeon is not usually classified as a strictly expository preacher, yet he frequently handled texts in an expository fashion. Who would ever suggest that

Spurgeon was not an expositor? Spurgeon preached an exceptional, textual expository message based on 1 Peter 2:24–25. He entitled his sermon, "The Sin Bearer" and developed it under three major headings and many subpoints: 1.) The Bearing of Our Sins by Our Lord, 2.) The Change in Our Condition, and 3.) The Healing of Our Diseases.[15] Just by reading the outline of this sermon, my soul is stirred; I understand why history has given Spurgeon the title "Prince of Preachers."

Expository, not Textual or Topical

I differentiate expository sermons from textual and topical sermons by defining expository preaching and contrasting it with typical textual and topical sermons. Distinct differences then emerge.

Expository preaching is the exposition of a passage (or passages) of Scripture, either short or long, based on a sound exegesis of the text. The passage is viewed within its contextual setting, organized around a dominant theme, illustrated for clarity, and applied compellingly to the hearers.

A textual sermon is based on a verse or two from the Bible, with the general theme of the sermon coming from the text. More often than not, the text is but a springboard into whatever the preacher wants to say. The preacher gets his general idea from the text and may expound it to some extent, but he feels no great responsibility to exegete the text or to place it in its contextual setting. One Southern Baptist theologian has described much Southern Baptist preaching as consisting solely of a "text and a tale." As a Southern Baptist pastor for over thirty years, I regret that there is too much truth for comfort in this man's observation. The evaluation can be applied not only to my own denomination but perhaps to most evangelical bodies in America today.

A topical sermon is built around a subject which may be taken from the Bible or outside of the Bible. The preacher may use the Scriptures to support his arguments, but he generally expresses his own views or the views of others. There is little of "Thus saith the Lord" in the average topical sermon. Sometimes no Scripture is used, and the end result is a glorified lecture rather than a true sermon. Freewheeling topics are explored in the pulpit today, from "How to Treat Your Mother-in-law" to "Nuclear Disarmament." One pastor told me that one of his favorite sermons was entitled, "The Anatomy of a Butterfly."

Haddon Robinson asserts that the difference in "topical exposition" and a "topical sermon" is that in topical exposition the thought of the Scripture must shape all that is said in developing the topic. This does not hold true for all topical sermons.[16]

True expository preaching must stay within

or expound the text of the Scriptures. A typical textual or topical sermon is not restricted to the scriptural material. The preaching of a purely textual or topical preacher may be described like this: 1.) He took a text, 2.) He departed therefrom, and 3.) He never returned.

Is there then, ever a place for a purely textual or topical sermon? Though I would not want to answer this question with an emphatic yes or no, I am compelled to assert my conviction that, for a sermon to be genuinely biblical, it must expound the Word of God and give the original meaning of the biblical writer in its context. Since this is true, much that is called preaching today is not biblical in this sense; such preaching is rather the religious insights and speculations of men.

Validity of Expository Preaching

Expository preaching protects the integrity of the preacher. In this day of much shame, pretense, and dishonesty, the preacher needs every encouragement toward personal integrity. I am greatly indebted to John R. W. Stott for these insights, but I have made them my own and added my own personal perception.

First, exposition sets limits for us, restricting us to the biblical text, since expository preaching is biblical preaching. Confinement to the scriptural text will prevent the preacher from making unfounded statements. Moreover, the best deterrent to heretical teaching is an antidote to subjective "off-the-wall" speculations and sound exposition. The proliferation of unbalanced teaching in our day would not have transpired if all preachers had been true expositors. As Ron Dunn suggested, there has been too much "speculating" and not enough "revelating" in our day.

Second, exposition demands integrity. The common saying that the Bible can be made to mean or say anything one desires is true only if one lacks integrity. The preacher of integrity will never juggle the text to suit his fancy. His major purpose is to speak what God has already spoken in his infallible Word.

The true expositor, according to Stott, will never be so forgetful of his text by departing from it and following his own fancy. Nor will he be disloyal to his text by appearing to remain with the text but by twisting it into something entirely different from its original meaning.[17]

An example of a crude, glaring lack of integrity came to my ears recently. A certain preacher was chided for driving a Cadillac automobile when Jesus rode a donkey. The preacher replied, "The donkey in the days of Jesus was like having a Cadillac. Very few people could afford a donkey and Jesus was one of them." To suggest that Jesus was rich enough to afford luxuries is false (see Matt. 8:20). The pastor making this statement is either deceptive or ignorant of the Scriptures.

Third, exposition gives us confidence to preach. If we are expounding our own views, we may not be able to speak with deep conviction. But if we are expounding God's imperishable, infallible Word with honesty and integrity, we are very bold. Amos the prophet said, "The Lord GOD has spoken! Who can but prophesy?" (Amos 3:8). Whoever speaks, wrote the apostle Peter, should do so, as one who utters "the oracles of God" (1 Pet. 4:11). Such is the privilege and grave responsibility of every expositor of the Word of the living God.

CHAPTER 4

The Biblical Foundations of Expository Preaching

The attitude of the preacher toward the Bible is absolutely crucial in expository preaching because expositional proclamation, in its very essence, is the proclamation of the written Word of God. John R. W. Stott says there are five great theological foundations for biblical preaching, namely, a conviction about God, the Scriptures, the church, the pastorate, and preaching. Stott's view is valid, but I am convinced that if one interprets the Scriptures correctly, then one will hold correct convictions about God, the church, the pastorate, and preaching.

Expository preaching is the preaching of the Holy Scriptures. True expository preaching is, therefore, possible only if one holds a high view of the Scriptures. What is critical in maintaining such a view?

Scripture Is God's Written Word

The expository preacher must believe that Scripture is God's Word written. What the Scriptures say, God says, for the Bible is God speaking. If Scripture handles the very words of the living God, "not in words which man's wisdom teaches but which the Holy Spirit teaches" (1 Cor. 2:13), then no trouble should be too great in its study and exposition. If, on the other hand, we believe the Bible is not trustworthy at certain points, our enthusiasm in studying and expounding diminishes greatly or is destroyed entirely. The true expositor must begin with the conviction that the Bible is both plenarily (see 2 Tim. 3:16) and verbally inspired (see 1 Cor. 2:13). The "Baptist Faith and Message," adopted by Southern Baptists in 1925 and 1963, expresses this high view of the Bible in its article on the Holy Scriptures: The Bible has "truth without any mixture of error for its matter" or content.

The expository method is of little use without the expository message. My homiletics professor, Dr. James Clelland, was an avid advocate of the expository method, while some of his colleagues denied the very authenticity of much of the Bible. I was thus faced with the dilemma of being trained *in* the expository method and being trained *out of* the expository message. In my case I opted to follow my homiletics professor but not my Bible professors. To put it bluntly, I believe the Bible is the inerrant Word of God and have preached it accordingly.

God Still Speaks Through His Word

The expository preacher must also believe that God still speaks through what He has spoken. Scripture is more than a collection of ancient documents in which the Word of God is preserved. On the contrary, Scripture is the living Word to living people from the living God, a contemporary message for the contemporary world.

For example, Jesus stated to Satan: "Man shall not live by bread alone, but by every word that proceeds from the mouth of God" (Matt. 4:4). Though quoting a word spoken by Moses thirteen hundred years before (see Deut. 8:3), Jesus declared that this very same word proceeds from God's mouth through the Scriptures *in the present* to give life. Paul asks, "Do you not hear the law?" (Gal. 4:21) and also, "What does the Scripture say?" (Gal. 4:30). These are extraordinary questions, for "the law" and "Scripture" are ancient writings. How can an old book "speak" in such a way that we can hear it speaking? Only in one way—God himself speaks through it and we can hear his voice.

This concept of the contemporary voice of God is notable, particularly in the epistle to the Hebrews (see 3:7,15). The author quotes Psalm 95, "Today, if you will hear His voice, do not harden your hearts" (Heb. 4:7). But he introduces the quotation with the words, in some translations, "as the Holy Spirit says." He thus implies that the Holy Spirit makes the same appeal to his people to listen as he made a thousand years earlier when the psalm was written.[1]

Another example of the living Word is found in the seven letters to the churches of Asia (see Rev. 2–3). Each letter ends with the entreaty, "He who has an ear, let him hear what the Spirit says to the churches." What John had written some time past, the Holy Spirit was still speaking with a living voice, even to every individual church member who had an ear to listen to his message.

With profound insight, Dr. Stott makes this observation concerning the living Word:

When once we have grasped the truth that God still speaks through what He has spoken, we shall be well protected against two opposite errors. The first is the belief that, though it was heard in ancient times, God's voice is silent today. The second is the claim that God is indeed speaking today, but that His Word has little or nothing to do with Scripture. The first leads to Christian antiquarianism, the second to Christian existentialism. Safety and truth are found in the related convictions that God has spoken, that God speaks, and that His messages are closely connected to one another because it is through what He spoke that He still speaks. He makes His living Word contemporary and relevant until we find ourselves back on the Emmaus Road with Christ Himself expounding the Scripture to us, and our hearts on fire. Another way of putting the same truth is to say that we must keep the Word of God and the Spirit of God together. For apart from the Spirit it is alien. I cannot express this theme better than by borrowing an expression which I have heard Dr. James I. Packer use: "Having studied the doctrine of Scripture for a generation," he has said, "the most satisfactory model is to describe it thus: The Bible is God speaking."[2]

God's Word Accomplishes God's Purposes

The expository preacher must believe God's Word accomplishes God's purposes. Not only has God spoken; not only does God continue to speak through what He has spoken, but when God speaks, he acts. "For the Word of God is living and powerful, and sharper than any two-edged sword, piercing even to the division of soul and spirit, and of joints and marrow, and is a discerner of the thoughts and intents of the heart" (Heb. 4:12). Therefore, the Word accomplishes whatever God sends it forth to do (see Isa. 55:11). God created the universe by his Word. He spoke and it came to be (see Ps. 33:9). Now through the same word and authority He recreates and saves. The gospel is God's power for salvation to everyone who believes; for it pleased God by the *kerugma,* the message proclaimed, to save those who believe (see Rom. 1:16 and 1 Cor. 1:21).

Many comparisons are used in the Bible to illustrate the powerful influence which the Word exerts. Like a hammer, the Word can break stony hearts. Like fire, it can burn up rubbish. The Word illumines our path, shining like a lamp on a dark night, and like a mirror, it shows us both what we are and what we should be. The Word is a seed causing birth, milk causing growth, wheat which strengthens, honey which sweetens, and gold which enriches its owner.[3]

Let me share a story. A preacher was passing through the security check at an airport. It was before the day of electronic scanning, and the security official was rummaging through his briefcase. He ran across a black cardboard box which contained the preacher's Bible. "What's in the box?" the official asked suspiciously. The preacher gave a startling reply, "Dynamite." Indeed, the Bible is dynamite because the God who spoke it speaks it again. A seminary classmate referred to the New Testament as TNT! To believe in the explosive power of God's Word should be enough in itself to make an effective preacher out of everyone who is called to preach.

An Inspired Legacy

Some say that one's view of the inspiration of the Scripture does not matter in preaching. As Andrew Blackwood wrote, "Fortunately a man's effectiveness in the pulpit does not depend upon his theory of inspiration."[4] I disagree with this esteemed professor of preaching. As Merrill Unger has said, "If the Bible is considered merely to contain the Word of God, rather than actually to be *en toto* the Word of God, there is naturally a decreased sense of responsibility to study its text minutely, or to systematize its theology, or authoritatively to declare its message."[5]

Three great Bible preachers in this century were almost lost to the ministry of the Word because at one time they doubted the authority of the Bible. But each of these men searched their souls and the Scriptures and came to a belief in the inerrancy of the entire Bible. These men were G. Campbell Morgan, Vance Havner, and Billy Graham. Just think of the great loss to our world had these men continued in unbelief concerning the Bible. Think, as well, of the unspeakable blessing that would suddenly descend upon this confused, lost, and frustrated world if every preacher believed that the Bible is "truth without mixture of error" and preached it with that conviction in the power of the Holy Spirit.

CHAPTER 5

The Nature of
Evangelistic Preaching

Christian preaching must be evangelistic because the good news of Jesus Christ, the *Evangel,* is the distinctive element in the Christian message.

Evangelistic preaching is here understood as the public proclamation of the gospel of Jesus Christ in the power of the Holy Spirit with the aim of making men disciples of Christ. It assumes a preacher—the evangelist; it takes for granted an audience; and it presupposes a place for preaching. A human being stands before fellow humans and declares to them the mighty redemptive acts of God in Christ.

Perhaps a more complete definition would read: Evangelistic preaching is presenting

Jesus Christ in the power of the Holy Spirit, that men may put their trust in God through him, accept him as their Savior, and serve him as their King, in the fellowship of his church. While no definition is completely adequate, any definition reveals the lofty nature of the task and the awesome responsibility of the evangelist.

The Presuppositions of Evangelistic Preaching

The principles of expository preaching which characterize any sermon should also mark the evangelistic sermon. However, some specific presuppositions, qualities, and techniques must undergird effective evangelistic preaching. Commitment to these fundamentals is vital for effective evangelistic proclamation.

All Lost without Jesus Christ

Paul describes the distressing condition of those without Christ as "having no hope and without God in the world" (Eph. 2:12). In other contexts, this hopelessness becomes eternal for those who die without a saving knowledge of the only Savior of humankind. "And anyone not found written in the Book of Life was cast into the lake of fire" (Rev. 20:15). "For the great day of His wrath has come, and who is able to stand?" (Rev. 6:17).

Do we really believe that men are lost—lost to themselves and lost to God? Do we believe that being lost will bring eternal separation from God in the life to come? Do we believe in the reality of hell for unbelievers? And do we really believe that Jesus Christ came "to seek and to save that which was lost?" (Luke 19:10).

The loftiest picture of God in Scripture, I believe, is found in Luke 15. In this context God is pictured as the Shepherd, the weeping woman, and the faithful Father—all seeking the souls of the lost. The only place in Scripture where God is shown "running" is when the Father races to meet the wayward prodigal (see Luke 15:20).

Dwight L. Moody was perhaps the greatest soul-winner since Paul. Why? His overwhelming conviction was that every person without Jesus Christ is lost. Moody said that whenever he looked at anyone, he saw either the letter *S* or *L* on his or her forehead. He saw them as Saved or Lost, and if Lost, he sought to win them to Jesus. William Booth was asked if he thought he had the best plan for developing soul-winners. He replied, "No, but I think my approach would be improved upon if I could lower each soul-winner into hell and let them experience the torments of the damned for a minute."

When the preacher believes that people are

71

lost, preaching halfheartedly or nonchalantly will be impossible. Rather the preacher will plead, entreat, and beseech in the confidence that some will be saved.

Jesus Christ—the Only Way to Salvation

The New Testament is abundantly clear in proclaiming that Jesus is "*the* way, the truth, and the life. No one comes to the Father except through Me" (John 14:6). Other religions offer ethical insights, but no Savior from sin and no assurance of heaven. Religion at its best is but humankind reaching up to God, while the gospel is God reaching down to man in the person of Jesus of Nazareth. "No one has seen God at any time. The only begotten Son, who is in the bosom of the Father, He has declared Him" (John 1:18). This "only begotten Son," Jesus Christ, became a human being, dwelt among mortals, died for their sins on the cross, and rose again to save them from their sins. Jesus Christ "was delivered up because of our offenses, and was raised because of our justification" (Rom. 4:25).

What made the apostle Paul so effective? Was it his intellect, his rhetoric, or his charisma? No, Paul modeled faith in the power of the gospel to save. Paul's declaration rings in our ears, "I am not ashamed of the gospel of Christ, for it is the power of God to salvation for everyone who believes" (Rom. 1:16). Armed with this conviction, any called person can preach evangelistic messages that will turn sinners to the Savior. Lacking this conviction, no one should even enter a pulpit to make an evangelistic appeal.

Preaching as God's Instrument for Salvation

No one expressed this truth so cogently as Paul when he wrote, "It pleased God through the foolishness of the message preached to save those who believe" (1 Cor. 1:21). "And how shall they believe in Him of whom they have not heard? And how shall they hear without a preacher?" (Rom. 10:14). Wherever the gospel of Jesus Christ has been preached, people are delivered from their sins and become the children of God.

Those who say that preaching has lost its power to save men do not understand the nature of Christian preaching. Dr. Vernon L. Stanfield, erstwhile professor of preaching at New Orleans Baptist Theological Seminary, describes true preaching as follows:

It is not a man sharing his own ideas, opinions or even interpretations. It is not a man standing before others parading knowledge or displaying his ability. Ideally, a Christian preacher is one who stands before his fellow men with God's message; he stands in God's stead and speaks for him. Christian preaching

73

is not even speech about God; it is God speaking. Of course, the preacher is not God, and his voice is not God's, but no man can justifiably accept the title, a herald of God, unless he declares, like the apostle Paul, that which he had first received. Where the mighty acts of God in Christ are proclaimed, there Christ will be to act again. The proclamation of the good news has been and will be God's chief means of saving men. Preaching and evangelism are inextricably bound together.[1]

The Lost Still Saved by the Preaching of the Word

Some have lost their faith in the converting power of preaching. They insist that the preaching service is only a "decision registration" time—the moment when people merely come forth to register prior decisions. Though regrettably that is true in most churches today, the effective evangelist believes that still other decisions will be made as he preaches the good news of salvation under the anointing of the Holy Spirit. Those who never witness the salvation of the lost when they preach should search their souls and examine their sermons to see what is lacking. Paul declared that when he preached something happened (see 1 Cor. 2:4). As the saying goes, when the apostle preached, there was either a revival or a riot.

A discouraged brother once said to D. L.

Moody, "I notice when you preach people make decisions, but when I preach there are no decisions." Moody replied, "Do you expect people to make decisions?" The answer came, "No." Then Moody said, "And that's the reason." The evangelist who does not believe persons will be saved when he preaches has not only lost his faith in preaching, but he also has lost his faith in the power of the gospel. The gospel "is the power of God to salvation for everyone who believes" (Rom. 1:16). "Faith comes by hearing, and hearing by the word of God" (Rom. 10:17). When you join these two unchanging truths together, you must conclude that preaching does indeed result in the salvation of souls.

Dr. Vernon L. Stanfield makes a strong case for the efficacy of evangelistic preaching. He writes,

> The Gospel of Christ has a mighty intrinsic power. When the Gospel is preached and when a man hears in faith, the power of the Gospel works and salvation is wrought in that man's heart. Perhaps we have sought to win lost people with our own methods and in our own wisdom. We may have begun almost unconsciously to believe in the power of techniques. But power comes from an Omnipotent God, who releases it when the good news concerning Jesus Christ is believed.[2]

The Content of Evangelistic Preaching

Someone has said, "Many people today are being saved before they even know they are lost." This statement bespeaks the tragedy of much so-called evangelistic preaching in our day. I talk to numerous persons about their experience of salvation. In my most recent soul-winning experience, I asked a lady who was troubled about her assurance, "What did you do on the night you professed Christ?" She replied, "I asked Jesus to come into my heart." Upon further questioning, I discovered that she had never been told that she was a lost sinner, that Jesus had died for her sins, that she needed to repent and trust Christ. When she did trust Christ, she was gloriously converted, and, like the healed man in Acts 3, she almost leaped with joy.

The good news of Jesus Christ, the *Evangel,* is the basis for the evangelistic message. What is the specific content for evangelistic preaching? The central message must include the following: 1.) The doctrine of grace, 2.) The doctrine of man, 3.) The doctrine of God, 4.) The doctrine of Christ, 5.) The doctrine of repentance and faith, 6.) The doctrine of the new birth, 7.) The doctrine of forgiveness, 8.) The doctrine of eternal life, and 9.) The doctrine of the lordship of Jesus Christ.

In the New Testament two basic messages

were proclaimed. First, the good news of the death, burial, and resurrection of Jesus Christ for the forgiveness of sins was called the *kerugma* (the Greek word for preaching). Second, the ethical teaching of the Christian faith was called the *didache* (the Greek word for teaching).

While the *kerugma* was the message to the non-Christian world, the *didache* was instruction to the church. The gospel embraces both the *kerugma* and the *didache,* and evangelistic preaching incorporates the two. Today, the evangelistic message must make central the saving grace of Jesus Christ in his death, burial, and resurrection, but it cannot omit stressing the quality of life expected of the confessing Christians.

The Goals of Evangelistic Preaching

Evangelistic preaching demands a verdict. If it does not, it is not evangelistic; it is just a lecture or good advice. What goals should the preacher have in mind? There are at least five important objectives.

Personal Trust in Jesus Christ as Savior and Lord

This trust must be from the heart and accompanied by genuine repentance from sin. "That if you confess with your mouth the Lord

Jesus and believe in your heart that God has raised Him from the dead, you will be saved. For with the heart one believes to righteousness, and with the mouth confession is made to salvation" (Rom. 10:9–10).

Public Acknowledgment of Commitment

The public invitation is often criticized, sometimes with validity when it manipulates, or even tricks, persons. However, we need not apologize for doing something so clearly taught in the Scriptures, provided we do not abuse it. Every person that Jesus called was called publicly. He even told Zaccheus to climb down from the tree and make his public decision. Jesus solemnly declares, "Therefore whoever confesses Me before men, him I will also confess before My Father who is in heaven. But whoever denies Me before men, him I will also deny before My Father who is in heaven" (Matt. 10:32–33). Paul said, "For with the heart one believes to righteousness, and with the mouth confession is made to salvation" (Rom. 10:10).

Making a profession of faith is not easy. The cost can be great; however, the open acknowledgment of our faith is the proof that salvation has been experienced on the inside. This act of confession seems to strengthen one's faith.

I preached in Cuba immediately after Castro came to power. One night I gave an invitation, and twenty-eight persons professed faith in Christ, a dangerous thing to do. As these twenty-eight persons stood before the congregation, an elderly member of the church stood to commend them for their courage. He then quoted the words of Jesus in Matthew 10:32–33. The next day one convert pulled me aside and said, "I received Jesus last night, and I fear it will cost me my relationship with my father and my priest." Opening his shirt, he showed me an idol of the Virgin Mary he wore. He said, "It is very hard for me to take this off my body. It has been such a vital part of my religion." But this convert confessed openly and in doing so, convinced me he really had met Jesus.

Baptism

The New Testament clearly teaches "believe, confess, and be baptized" in this order. When Paul was converted, his first question was "Lord, what do you want me to do?" (Acts 9:6) not "What do others want me to do, or what would I like to do?" The very first thing a new convert should do is to follow the command of Jesus and be baptized. Some would insist that we should wait until the new convert proves he is truly a child of God. No, we should trust the testimony of the new believer and follow the example of the apostolic church. After all, baptism is not a confession of sanctification but of justification, not a completion but a beginning of our Christian experience.

On the Day of Pentecost three thousand souls were saved and on the same day three thousand souls were baptized (Acts 2:38–41). The time to tell a new Christian to be baptized is when he is truly saved. If you wait, that person may never obey Christ in baptism; and if he fails in this initial obedience, how can we have assurance he will honor Jesus in other areas of his life? Jesus is Lord, and this means baptism is not negotiable for the true believer.

Church Membership

Evangelism is not complete until the new convert is in the fellowship of the church.[3] The New Testament, said John Wesley, knows nothing of a solitary Christian. The word *saint* does not appear once in the New Testament; it is always "saints." And those who were saved in the New Testament were added to the church.

History has shown that where there is no emphasis on commitment to church membership, the fruits of evangelism are usually lost. For example, the Jesus Movement in the 1960s and early 1970s placed no stress on church membership. Where are the followers of this movement today? Most of them have been lost to Christ and the church. The church is God's university for training the converts; He has no other plan. The evangelistic preacher ought to honor it.

Coercion should not be used to persuade the new convert to be baptized or to affiliate with the local church; rather each one's particular circumstances must be considered compassionately. The ideal goal is still both baptism and church membership.

Personal Witnessing

The task of evangelism is not completed until the evangelized becomes an evangelist. Jesus commands us to teach new converts everything He has taught us (see Great Commission in Matt. 28:18–20). If there is one thing the Master teaches us, it is for us to witness constantly. Peter Wagner says that unless a new convert is taught to witness within two years following salvation, few will ever become witnesses. Therefore, the new Christian should be challenged with the privilege and responsibility of witnessing from the day he is saved. While this challenge is mainly the responsibility of the pastor, the evangelist initiates it at the time of salvation.

Expository preaching lays the foundation for evangelistic preaching. The most powerful evangelistic messages are expository in nature and follow the rules for expository preaching given in this book. The most effective way to show the absolute necessity for the new birth is to expound the third chapter of John, showing Nicodemus as a typical and sincere religious person but without the reality of Christ in his life. The expository method of evangelistic preaching, rather than the topical sermon, allows the person of Nicodemus to come alive for congregations. When men and women hear the message of the gospel preached this way, they will be moved by its power and commit their lives to follow Christ.

CHAPTER 6

An Evaluation: Expository and Evangelistic Preaching

The Expository Method Evaluated

The advantages to the expository method in preaching can be considered from the standpoint of both the preacher and the people. Some alleged disadvantages of the expository approach must be considered as well.

Advantages for the Preacher

Authority and Power   When the preacher stands to speak, he knows he is delivering God's message, not his own. He speaks, yet the glorious truth is, God at the same time is speaking through him. As Jerry Vines so aptly puts it, "He is merely the mouth and lips through which the living Word of God is conveyed to the congregation."[1]

An Inexhaustible Source of Material There is no dearth of preaching material for the man who preaches the Bible. A distressed preacher came to John Dick, the well-known professor of theology, and said, "What shall I do? I have preached all I know to my people and have nothing else to give them. I have gone through the catechism and what have I more?" To which John Dick replied, "The catechism! Take the Bible, man. It will take you a long time to exhaust that."[2] A young preacher asked me, "What is the best book of sermons you have ever read?" I replied, "The Holy Bible"; I was not being sarcastic.

No One-subject Fixation Expository preaching saves the preacher from riding hobby horses, from a one-subject mentality such as sermon after sermon on the Second Coming, the Holy Spirit, or biblical authority. True expository preaching helps keep the preacher from over emphasizing pet subjects.[3]

Enriched Knowledge of God's Word The preacher who faithfully exegetes the Word week by week will learn the truth of the Bible. If, on the other hand, he uses the hop-skip-and-jump approach, he cannot expect to master the Bible. I never really grasped the full sweep of the Bible until I began to expound books of the Bible, the great chapters of the Bible, and other large sections of Scripture. To preach through Romans, Genesis, or Revelation helps one to comprehend the whole Bible.

Not a Weapon   Expository preaching keeps the preacher from using the Bible as a club. Men and women cannot stand to be "preached at." But when the text of Scripture says in effect, "You are the one," no reasonable person can complain.

Personal Discipline   The serious expositor of the Word of God will study hard and consistently. He cannot "goof off" and prepare expository messages week by week. Exposition of the Scriptures gives the preacher a built-in plan of discipline.

Time-saver   Some preachers spend half the week looking for something to preach; I too have been guilty of this. The expositor, in most cases, is able to begin serious study and exegesis of his text early in the week.

Nourishment for the Soul   Before he feeds his people, the preacher must feed himself. In fact, the preacher should benefit more from the Word he proclaims than his people do. God commanded Ezekiel to eat and fill his soul with the sweetness of the Word. Only then was he to share that Word with his people (see Ezek. 3:3–4). Haddon Robinson says, "A preacher must learn to listen to God before he speaks for Him."[4]

Advantages for the People

Spiritual Needs Met   Jesus said, "Man shall not live by bread alone, but by every word that proceeds from the mouth of God" (Matt. 4:4). People on a steady diet of Bible preaching will find themselves gradually conforming to the image of God's Son. "As newborn babes, desire the pure milk of the word, that you may grow [into salvation]" (1 Pet. 2:2). Also, constantly hearing the Word is a deterrent to sin. "Your word I have hidden in my heart, That I might not sin against You" (Ps. 119:11). The Word in the heart will also produce great peace in the soul and a peaceful attitude toward others. "Great peace have those who love Your law, and nothing causes them to stumble" (Ps. 119:165). Moreover, the hearing of the Word will increase one's faith. "So then faith comes by hearing, and hearing by the word of God" (Rom. 10:17).

Study of Word Encouraged   When people hear the marvels of the Word unfolded, they want more of the Word for themselves. They, therefore, seek out the Truth, just as the Berean Christians "received the word with all readiness, and searched the Scriptures daily to find out whether these things were so" (Acts 17:11). When laypersons competently interpret Scripture, the church approaches maturity.

Vision Increased "Where there is no revelation, the people cast off restraint" (Prov. 29:18). Generally, where there is no vision, the people have little grasp of the broad sweep of divine revelation. When they do grasp the fullness of the Word, the greatness of God and the greatness of His plan for the individual, the church, and the world is revealed. Expository preaching enables the people of God to make this wonderful discovery.

Equipping for Service Good expository preaching will challenge the people to be "doers of the word, and not hearers only" (James 1:22). The result is an obedient army of the redeemed to serve the Lord through local churches. Teachers, preachers, missionaries, soul-winners, and prayer warriors are the products of Bible preaching.

Growth into the Likeness of Christ Expository preaching delivers big doses of the Word. As the people feed constantly on this diet of divine truth, they are growing into full salvation (see 1 Pet. 2:2) which is the likeness of Christ (see 2 Cor. 3:18). Thus expository preaching is a primary means by which God accomplishes his ultimate purpose for his children.

Disadvantages of Expository Preaching

I have extolled the advantages of expository preaching for both pastor and people. What are its alleged disadvantages?

Laziness   Some lazy men, no doubt, have chosen expository preaching to avoid a lot of hard work. They select a passage and chatter away for half an hour on the ideas suggested in the text. They may call this expository preaching, but it is nothing of the kind.[5] The expository method is not for the lazy man. If one thinks he can do expository preaching without work, he is not doing expository preaching. Dr. Douglas White asserts, "The fact of the business is that, far from being a labor saving device, it involves far more laborious effort on the part of the preacher than any other type."[6]

No Variety   The charge is made that expository preaching is dull, always the same old thing, with no up-to-date application to people's needs. This is true of some expository preaching. I have sat in audiences, bored stiff, while some dull preacher delivered his "masterpiece." Dullness is not the fault of the method, however; rather, the problem lies in the shabby preparation and delivery of the preacher himself. The problem may lie in the fact that the preacher has no anointing of the Holy Spirit upon his life. Or, to quote Haddon Robinson, "Dull expository preaching usually lacks creative applications."[7]

Not Led by the Spirit   Some expositors are so bound to a routine that they give no place to the Holy Spirit. The Sunday following the bombing of Pearl Harbor, we are told, most preachers did not even mention the dastardly event. I know a preacher who said he preached on Jezebel on Mother's Day; another expounded on Job on Christmas Day. The wise expositor is never enslaved to a pattern he cannot change. He will select his text according to the voice of the Holy Spirit and the needs of the hour.

Mere Commentary   Reading verses and making comments, though often done, is not expository preaching. Expository preaching calls for the utmost preparation in the most comprehensive way. The power of expository preaching lies in its focus on one central theme and its development by sound exegesis and relevant application. A mere commentary on verses is just the opposite.

No Clear Plan   If the preaching has no clear outline, such is not true exposition. Expository sermons are built around a dominant theme and an outline derived directly from the text.

Too Many Details Burdening a sermon with too many details is undoubtedly a temptation for some expositors; the Puritans often drowned their people in an ocean of facts. Pertinent details are important, however. At times it may be helpful to bring in the original languages, but "technical baggage" should not be brought into the pulpit. Give the people the cream of your study. Do not beat them to death with excessive material. Drive for the main lesson of the passage. Give them the big picture. Do not weary them with small and insignificant details.

Irrelevant Issues Expository preaching may not address relevant issues. On the contrary, true exposition indeed does apply the truth to the needs of the hearers. Dr. Haddon Robinson writes,

> Seldom do people lose sleep over the Jebusites, the Canaanites, the Perizzites, or even over what Abraham or Moses might have said or done. They lie awake wondering about grocery prices, crop failures, quarrels with girlfriends, diagnosis of a malignancy, frustrated sex life, or the rat race which only the rats seem to win. If the sermon does not make much difference in that world, they wonder if it makes any difference at all.[8]

The Evangelistic Method Evaluated

Because the expository method of preaching lays the foundation for evangelistic preaching, the advantages both to the preacher and to the people of evangelistic preaching are quite similar. Like expository preaching, evangelistic preaching gives the preacher an opportunity to preach with power and authority, as long as he is proclaiming the message of the gospel, in the power of the Holy Spirit.

The advantage of evangelistic preaching for the people is that they must have an evangelistic preacher who will proclaim to them this saving message. Without Jesus Christ, men and women are lost in sin, and they need to be saved from their sins. The apostle Paul promises, "Whoever calls upon the name of the Lord shall be saved" (Rom. 10:13). One might read this statement and conclude that all he needed to do to be saved is to say a prayer. Not true. Before one can call upon the Lord he must believe. And before he can believe he must hear the bad news of his lostness and the good news that Jesus Christ died and rose again to redeem him.

The evangelistic preacher proclaims the necessity for all to be saved; such is the highest expression of preaching. It is unconscionable that any person truly called to preach would not preach the good news of salvation. The apostle Paul continues in Romans 10:14–15 to assert the priority and privilege of evangelistic preaching: "How then shall they call on Him in whom they have not believed? And how shall they believe in Him of whom they have not heard? And how shall they hear without a preacher?" (Rom. 10:14).

PART THREE

The Word Goes Forth

CHAPTER 7

Armed in Spirit, Body, and Soul

The preacher's first and most important task is to prepare himself, not his sermon, and anyone who has spent a few years in the ministry will agree wholeheartedly about this. A young preacher tends to think the primary concern is to prepare the sermon; but far more important is the preparation of the preacher himself. As Dr. Haddon Robinson has ably stated, "The audience does not primarily hear a sermon but a man."[1]

The preacher needs to prepare his total person—his spirit, his body, and his mind—for maximum benefit.

The Spirit

The preacher prepares his spirit primarily through two disciplines: Bible study and prayer. Every preacher should read through the Bible once every year at a minimum. Let me make several suggestions about Bible reading.

Bible Reading

Read Your Bible Systematically Do not read at random. If you do, you will read only your favorite passages and will get a lopsided view of the Scriptures. This could lead to a serious imbalance in your spiritual life and even to heresy.

Devise a Yearly Plan of Bible Reading There are several plans for reading the Bible through each year. Use one of these or develop a plan of your own. I have devised several plans through the years for the members of the churches I have served. Once you devise a plan, hold yourself accountable to completing the task. At the present time I am using *The One Year Bible,* published by Tyndale House and based on the New International Version. *The One Year Bible* has been prepared especially for those who wish to read the Bible through in one year in a very readable and accurate modern translation. In this plan for 365 days, the reader has a passage from the Old Testament, one from the New Testament, one from the Psalms, and one or two Proverbs. At the end of the year you will have read once through the entire Old Testament, covering Psalms twice, and once through the New Testament.

Read the Bible to Feed Your Own Soul   Do not read the Bible merely to find texts for sermons. Read it as the food God provides for your soul's nourishment, growth, and well-being. Before Ezekiel was in a position to speak God's Word to his people, he had to devour and digest the Word himself. "And He said to me: 'Son of man, I am sending you to the children of Israel, to a rebellious nation that has rebelled against Me; they and their fathers have transgressed against Me to this very day'" (Ezek. 2:3). Jeremiah exulted in the Word of the Lord, declaring, "Your words were found, and I ate them, and Your word was to me the joy and rejoicing of my heart" (Jer. 15:16). The psalmist found God's Word tasted sweeter than honey, exclaiming, "How sweet are Your words to my taste, Sweeter than honey to my mouth" (Ps. 119:103). I have found that when I feasted on the Word myself, then my people feasted on the word I delivered from the pulpit. My preacher father used to say to me, "If you are blessed by the Word, then your people will be blessed. But if you are not blessed yourself, no one else will be blessed."

Stop When the Scriptures Especially Speak to You   As you read along, certain verses

97

will hit you, speak to you, and suggest a sermon. When this occurs, stop and write down the verse or thought which came to mind. You will soon find you have accumulated a pile of sermons. I have found this to be one of the richest sources for sermon ideas.

Prayer

Bible study and prayer go hand in hand; they are spiritual twins. Prayer is an absolute essential in the preacher's life. Read the biographies of the greatest preachers throughout the centuries, and you will find prayer has always been the great common denominator of their lives. John Wesley said he thought very little of a man who did not pray four hours a day. Robert Murray McCheyne died at the age of twenty-nine, yet the impact of his life was far greater than that of most men who live long lives. The secret of his remarkable life was prayer. It was McCheyne who said, "A calm hour with God is worth a lifetime with men."

As you carry out your commitment to pray, keep in mind the following suggestions.

Set a Time Each Day, Preferably at the Beginning of the Day, to Pray   Prayer must not be left to our feeling or convenience. A specific time to pray will encourage us to pray daily whether we feel like it or not. The effectiveness of our praying does not depend upon the way we feel, but upon the faithfulness of God.

Pray Without Ceasing   Prayer should not be confined only to mornings or other set times; prayer should be constant throughout the day. Our prayers need not be long. They can be brief, just a few words at a time—what some have called "arrow prayers." Jesus often prayed very brief prayers, even sentence prayers at times. Paul commands us to "pray without ceasing" (1 Thess. 5:17). This does not mean we should be perpetually on our knees but that we should always be in a spirit of prayer. However, do not let your praying through the day keep you from that special time reserved only to pray.

Obey Every Impulse to Pray   The impulse to pray may come when you are reading, driving your car, jogging, or as you are battling a text. When that impulse comes, always obey it. It is the will of the Holy Spirit. By responding to this impulse, you will have some of your greatest experiences in prayer.

I have found it very helpful to make an agenda for each day's activities. At the top of the agenda I always write down the letters "GTWF," meaning Get in touch with the Father. This is a directive to me to begin the day with prayer, no matter how pressing the demands upon my time may be. During this sacred time I generally pray about thirty minutes. I utter a brief word of prayer in the midst of other activities. Sometimes I go aside to pray longer. My most precious times in prayer have come when the Holy Spirit awakens me in the middle of the night to pray. Often I have found myself praying for an hour or more as the Holy Spirit moved in my heart. Using the Lord's Prayer as a guide, I have greatly enriched and enlarged my praying. In January of 1986, I preached six sermons on the subject "Could You Not Tarry with Me One Hour?" In these messages I shared the ingredients one might possibly use in an hour-long prayer. These messages are on tape and available through our Media Ministry in Houston, Texas.

The Body

The believer's body is the temple of the Holy Spirit, but it is also the place where we "live and move and have our being" (Acts 17:28). This temple should be kept in the best possible condition. The better the physical condition of our bodies, the better we can serve the Lord.

Several essentials are necessary for the health of the body, including exercise, proper diet, and rest.

Exercise

The exercise program you follow must be personal. You may choose to jog, walk, swim, or play some sport. In 1960 I discovered I was growing sluggish. I would fall asleep in my chair when I tried to study. I felt tired much of the time. Providentially, I believe, my wife gave me a health club membership, and I began jogging. It was a miserable chore.

The first few times I jogged I covered only one fourth of a mile, and it seemed I had run five miles. But I kept on jogging until I got up to one mile per day and then two miles per day. At the present time I am jogging and walking for about fifty minutes, six times a week. In a short time I found my vitality restored. My mental alertness increased greatly. I felt stronger than I did when I was much younger. I do not enjoy jogging, but I do enjoy the positive benefits it brings. Jogging does not take much time; it does not require any money; you can do it anywhere; you can do it alone or with others; you can make your own rules; and it gives you excellent physical exercise. Somebody asked, "Why do you jog?" I answered, "I jog because I'm running from my funeral and running for my life."

Choose the exercise that fits you. But choose something and stay with it. It is the will of God for every preacher, unless he is physically unable.

Diet

Charles Finney said that "overeating" was the greatest sin of preachers in his day. Times have not changed! The average pastor is confronted with many opportunities to overeat. He must discipline himself in not overeating and in eating the right kinds of food. A good balanced diet, meeting his daily requirements from the various food groups, should keep the average pastor's weight down. Eat plenty of green, leafy vegetables. Be sure to eat enough bulk.

Three habits should be avoided like rattlesnakes regarding food: Do not snack between meals, do not eat late at night, and eat only a small amount of sweets and breads. An overweight preacher is a poor testimony to the power of the gospel in the preacher's own life. Every preacher would do well to heed Paul's resolve: "Like an athlete I punish my body, treating it roughly, training it to do what it should, not what it wants to. Otherwise I fear that after enlisting others for the race, I myself might be declared unfit and ordered to stand aside" (1 Cor. 9:27 TLB).

Rest

The body must have adequate rest to function properly. The body of the preacher especially needs to be rested before he delivers his sermon. The average preacher expends as much energy in preaching one sermon as a worker does in eight hours of work.

The body is God's vehicle to communicate

102

his saving message to men. Keep your body in good condition. Make your body a finely tuned tool for God.

An apocryphal story recounts that a young hunter from Ephesus entered the house of the apostle John, carrying an unstrung bow in his hand. He found the elderly apostle engaged in playing with a tame dove. The young man expressed astonishment that the apostle should be so involved with mundane things. John gently asked the young man why he carried his bow unstrung. The hunter replied that it was only in this way that the bow would retain its elasticity. "Even so," said John, "mind and body will not retain its elasticity or usefulness unless they are at times unstrung." Spend time "unstringing yourself." It will improve your sermon preparation and your sermon delivery.

The Mind

The effective expositor needs a trained mind in addition to his spiritual anointing. As Charles Koller cleverly put it, "A preacher must not preach out of the fullness of his heart and the emptiness of his head."

The parameters of acceptable fields of study are boundless. Certain studies are more valuable to the preacher than others. If you would communicate God's Word effectively to this generation, you will find some subject areas very profitable.

The Arts and Sciences

Every preacher needs a broad, general education in the arts and sciences. He needs basic studies such as English, history, literature, science, math, government, and philosophy. Such training gives the preacher a broad understanding of life and a perspective from which he can prepare and deliver his message. Dr. Haddon Robinson correctly asserts, "We must preach to a world addressed by the novelist, the columnist and the playwright. If we do not, we will have hearers who are orthodox in their head but heretics in their conduct."[2]

The Biblical Languages

There is tremendous value in being able to read the language of the Old Testament (Hebrew) and the language of the New Testament (Greek). Many language helps are available today. W. E. Vines' *Expository Dictionary of New Testament Words,* Kenneth Wuest's *Word Studies of the New Testament,* and A. T. Robertson's *Word Pictures in the New Testament* are most helpful to one who cannot read Hebrew or Greek. However, aids leave the preacher dependent on secondary sources. Going to the original tongues to find the truth in the Scriptures is exciting. Joy and confidence develop in preaching when the preacher is his own interpreter of God's Word. One need not know

Greek and Hebrew to preach effectively; there is, however, a great advantage in knowing the original languages. No preacher should fail to study them if it is at all possible.

Let me give a word of caution. Do not flaunt your knowledge of Greek and Hebrew. Keep them in the background. They are but tools for preparing the spiritual meal; they are not the meal itself. Suppose you are invited to a good meal in the home of a friend. Your hostess obviously used many tools to prepare a delicious meal for you. When you sit down to eat, she serves only the food and keeps the tools hidden away in the kitchen. So it should be with Greek and Hebrew.

Church History

Many regard history as a maze of dull events, persons, and dates from the past with no meaning for us in the present. Nothing could be further from the truth. Next to the Bible and the Holy Spirit, history is our greatest teacher. Church history is especially valuable for the preacher, for it shows him the terrible danger of falling into heresy and other errors. There are no new heresies; history recounts all of them and how they were propagated by very earnest men. When the preacher knows his history, he can spot heresy and avoid it. Without a historical perspective, he is subject to fall into heresy without realizing anything has happened to him. This is just one example of the value of knowing church history. Time will not permit us to enumerate other benefits here.

History of Revivals

The history of revivals shows how God intervened to bring spiritual awakenings when society had sunk to its lowest spiritual level. Preachers need to know how the Sovereign God has demonstrated his power in such times. Such knowledge can be the best antidote to discouragement and depression.

Biography

Study the lives of the great preachers. I recommend Warren Wiersbe's great book, *Walking with the Giants*. The "giants" are the great preachers of the ages. Study their lives and their preaching, and you will find much inspiration and information for your preaching. And you will find a source of spiritual challenge to your own life exceeded only by the Holy Scriptures.

Biblical and Systematic Theology

The expositor of the Scriptures should be trained in theology, both biblical and systematic. Biblical theology will enable him to see the very mind of God in the vast sweep of the Scriptures. Systematic theology will give the preacher a grasp of the great Bible doctrines and an understanding of their relationship with one another.

Biblical Interpretation

Study the principles and history of biblical interpretation. Hermeneutics will show the importance of understanding the Scripture in context and comparing Scripture with Scripture. Also it will acquaint the preacher with sound rules of biblical interpretation. Such a study should help the preacher avoid bizarre ideas and off-the-wall interpretations. Many of the popular errors that flourish in Christendom today are due to an ignorance of sound principles of biblical interpretation. It has been said that the Bible can be made to say anything you want; however, this could never be said of one who follows the rules of biblical interpretation.

Sermon Preparation and Delivery

Preachers are called by God, not made by man. But once called, a preacher can receive great benefits from a good course in sermon preparation and delivery. When I began to preach, I had never had one lesson in sermon preparation or delivery. What a joy to my heart when I was shown how I could derive an outline from a text and develop my thoughts around it. I am sure my congregation was more grateful than I. I believe the most difficult, and yet the most valuable, seminary course I ever had was a course in homiletics taught by a great Scottish homiletician, Dr. James Clelland. He made me "sweat blood" as he endeavored to teach me the art of sermon preparation and delivery. I have thanked the Lord many times for this course.

Current Events

The preacher should stay abreast of the world by reading a good daily newspaper. He should stay abreast of theology by reading a good theological magazine, such as *Christianity Today, The Christian Century* (liberal but provocative), *Biblioteca Sacra, The Theological Educator, or Moody Monthly*. He should buy good current books by outstanding evangelical authors on vital subjects. Obviously a busy pastor cannot read all the significant titles coming off the press. In such cases I have found it most helpful to read good reviews of current books.

Regardless of one's past education, the preacher should spend all the days of his ministry studying and preparing himself to be a more effective communicator of God's Word. Someone has said, "When you cease to sow in your study, you will cease to reap in your pulpit."

I wish also to warn of one danger in much reading and studying: The preacher may be tempted to let others do his thinking. You have probably met the preacher whose theology was the latest book he had read. So when the preacher studies, he should be his own thinker, his own interpreter, and his own theologian. Remember the old adage, "I milk a lot of cows, but I make my own butter."

The Preacher's Tools for Study

Like the carpenter, the preacher must have certain tools in order to do his work. Let me suggest several essential tools for the expositor.[3]

Bibles   I keep a King James Version of the Bible on my desk at all times. I have done most of my memorization from this version, and I read from it in the pulpit. In addition, I have all the other translations in English. I refer most often to the *New American Standard Version* (the most accurate modern translation, I believe) and the *New International Version* (the most readable modern translation). I highly recommend Howard Williams' translation of the New Testament because it describes so accurately the action of the Greek verbs. I also recommend *The Amplified New Testament* to those who don't know Greek. It is more like a concise commentary than a translation, but it brings out the meaning of the original Greek.

Paraphrases   I do not recommend paraphrases for basic study of the biblical text. I do find that a paraphrase will often give a beautiful insight into certain passages. For example, J. B. Phillips' paraphrase of Romans 12:1–2 and Ephesians 6:12 brings out the powerful messages in these crucial texts. Multiple translations are also helpful, such as Curtis Vaughan's *Twenty-six Translations of the New Testament*.

Concordances   The two best known concordances are those compiled by James Strong and Robert Young. An exhaustive concordance will enable you to discover all the places that an English word is used in the Bible. Both Strong and Young also have a system for discovering the Hebrew, Greek, or Aramaic word that was the basis of the translation. Properly used, they are marvelous tools.

Bible Dictionaries   The *Westminster Dictionary* is scholarly. The *Zondervan Pictoral Bible Dictionary* is written in a more popular style, but is a good, recent conservative work. Dictionaries have a wealth of information about people, places, institutions, terms, and customs.

No serious student would want to be without a good one.

Bible Atlases   Knowing the geography of the Bible helps you understand and interpret the Scripture. Archaeological discoveries have thrown much light on the geography and the political boundaries of the nations mentioned in the Bible. The location and historical development of both cities and nations are important to the expositor. For this you need a good Bible atlas.

Word Studies   W. E. Vines' *Expository Dictionary of the New Testament Words* is a valuable work. A. T. Robertson's *Word Pictures in the New Testament* is a classic, but hard to follow at points. Though not strictly word studies, William Barclay's Bible studies on the New Testament are full of valuable information not to be found anywhere else in such a readable form. His studies give much insight into the meaning of words.

Commentaries and Expositions   Two large sets of books have been very helpful to me: Alexander Maclaren's *Expositions of the Holy Scriptures* and G. Campbell Morgan's *The Westminster Pulpit*. These two sets are not, in reality, commentaries; they are powerful expository sermons. Any preacher will enrich his preaching from studying them. Rather than massive commentary sets, I prefer buying individual volumes on specific books of the Bible. For example, John Phillips' commentary on Romans, John Walvoord on Revelation, W. O. Carver and H. A. Ironside on Ephesians, Leo Eddleman on Acts, Henry Morris on Genesis, Paul Rees on Philippians, and Martin Loyd-Jones on the Sermon on the Mount have been rich resources for my preaching.

CHAPTER 8

Preparing Expository Sermons

Expository sermons must be prepared before they can be preached. Some preachers are either too lazy, too proud, or too pious to prepare their sermons.[1] Whatever the cause for lack of preparation, it must be overcome if one aspires to be an expositor. The preacher who would faithfully preach God's Word, using the expository method, must be prepared to spend many exacting hours each week in sermon preparation. Alexander Maclaren has been acclaimed by some as the greatest expositor in history. The reason is not hard to find: He shut himself in his study every day and devoted many hours to the preparation of each sermon.

One pious brother said he did not prepare

his sermons because of the assurance of Jesus in Matthew 10:19–20, "But when they deliver you up, do not worry about how or what you should speak. For it will be given to you in that hour what you should speak; for it is not you who speak, but the Spirit of your Father who speaks in you." What this brother failed to do was read this Scripture in its context. When read in context, the message is, "When they deliver you up (in court, not in church) you will be dragged before governors and kings for my sake. In such a situation you will not have time to prepare for your defense. It is then that the Holy Spirit will give you words to speak." Jesus' promise has brought great comfort to prisoners who lacked a counsel for the defense. But it offers no comfort to preachers who are either too lazy, too proud, or too pious to prepare to preach.

Psalm 81:10 has also been misinterpreted: "Open your mouth wide, and I will fill it." One brother read this verse and decided to try it out the next time he preached. He stood to preach, opened his mouth, and his mouth was indeed filled with hot air! One preacher who did not study was chiding another preacher for studying. "I don't study to preach," he said. "I just get in the pulpit, and the Holy Spirit fills me." The preacher who studied asked, "What if the Holy Spirit doesn't fill you?" The other replied, "I just mess around until He does." A lot of congregations can testify that much

114

messing around is going on and not enough preaching.[2]

Martyn Loyd-Jones doubted that preaching can be taught.[3] But I agree with Erasmus who said, "If elephants can be trained to dance, lions to play and leopards to hunt, surely preachers can be taught to preach." Certainly preachers are born, not made. However, if a man is a born preacher, he can be taught much about preaching which will be invaluable to him, especially in the area of sermon preparation.

While every preacher has to work out his own method of preparation, most of us find it necessary to take the following steps, which I've described using the insights of others, as well as my own experiences.

Step 1: Choose Your Text

The text is fundamental. We are expositors, not speculators. There is but *one* source of texts for the true expositor: the Bible. Yet there are many ways the preacher arrives at his specific text from the Bible.

A text will be found in the book of the Bible we are expounding. Perhaps a text may come from our regular devotional study of the Bible. John Stott writes, "If we are regular Bible students, then our memory becomes like a well-stocked food cupboard, and Biblical texts are lining up asking to be preached on."[4] I have a

file in my study labeled "Sermons Cooking."
This file contains sermon ideas or outlines
which have jumped out at me as I read the
Bible. I generally have from fifty to one hundred sermons "cooking" all the time. Of
course, in my beginning years, I had very little
cooking, except my sermon for the next Sunday. Many times I despaired in attempting to
produce two sermons a week. Now, the years
are shorter and the "cooking" file is thicker.

Many texts come to mind when you pray.
The Holy Spirit will often burden our hearts, as
he did the prophets, with a Word from the Lord
for our people.

A text may come from the seasons of the
year. The great landmarks of the Christian
calendar suggest basic themes. Palm Sunday,
Good Friday, Easter, Pentecost, and Christmas
also suggest their distinctive texts. In addition, national holidays often suggest our text.
At First Baptist Church, Ft. Smith, Arkansas,
we observed "special days" throughout the
year, and on those days I expounded relevant
biblical passages. I am doing the same at
Houston Northwest Baptist in Houston, Texas.

A text may emerge from a contemporary
event. The abortion issue, mounting suicides,
women's rights, divorce, war and peace, and
drug abuse are a few examples.

A text could come from known or revealed
needs of the congregation. The sensitive pastor will observe the needs of his people, and

the Holy Spirit reveals needs the pastor does not see. If the pastor mingles with his people, they will divulge areas he needs to address.

A text may emerge from our experience. My greatest joy has been to experience the truth of a text in my soul and then share it with my people from the pulpit. I recently discovered how to find and claim a biblical promise for myself. I was able to share this truth with my people with overflowing joy. My father, a pastor himself, often said to me, "Son, if you expect others to be blessed in your preaching, you must first be blessed yourself." A man said to Joseph Parker, "I want to thank you for that sermon. It did me good." Dr. Parker replied, "Sir, I preached it because it had done me good."[5] The greatest sermons are incarnated. The proverb is trite but tritely true which says, "It is better to see a sermon any day than to hear one."

A text may be seen or heard. My homiletics professor said, "A good preacher has homiletical ears and eyes." He can see a sermon on a billboard. He may see or hear a sermon idea on television. Most of us would call this vivid imagination. Whatever you call this gift, it makes for exciting preaching.

A text may suddenly be revealed from heaven and often the sermon to go with it. A homiletical proverb says, "Sermons that come down are better than those you work up." I do not mean to imply that prepared sermons do not come from above. I have never depended upon such direct revelations for my sermons, but they have come to me at times. I was jogging recently and began to reflect on the three pictures Jesus paints of God in Luke 15. Before I had finished my thirty minutes of jogging, a compelling sermon had filled my soul, which I titled "I Saw the Heart of God Today." The next Sunday I laid aside my prepared sermon and preached on that subject with great excitement. To me, that is the ultimate experience in preaching.

Permit me a word of personal experience that has helped me immensely in sermon preparation and delivery. During the first years of my ministry, when I was not so busy with administrative details, I spent many hours committing portions of the Bible to memory, especially the New Testament. As a result, I can often quote my text when I begin to prepare my message. I can also often recall other Scriptures which relate to the main theme and which are needed to support my argument.

When I was undergoing the ordeal of memorizing the Bible, I found it time consuming. However, through the years I have discovered that my memory of the Scriptures has been a tremendous timesaver. In my judgment you will find no exercise so helpful down the long road of sermon preparation as the memorization of Scriptures. I especially recommend

118

Scripture memorization to young men beginning in the ministry.

Step 2: Meditate on the Text

Read the text, re-read it, re-read it, and then read it again. Memorize it if it is not too long. Taste its nectar as a hummingbird delights in a flower. Wrestle with it like a dog does a bone. Chew it as a cow chews her cud. In this connection, Spurgeon wrote, "I always find I can preach best when I manage to lie asoak in my text . . . after I have bathed in it, I delight to lie down in it, and let it soak into me."[6] Campbell Morgan read his text fifty times before he would preach from it.[7]

Let me suggest a practical way to do this. Address three questions to your text: 1.) What did it mean when written, 2.) What does it mean now, and 3.) What does it mean to me and others personally?

As you answer the three questions, you may need to turn to a lexicon, concordance, or commentary. But these should never be more than aids. They should never replace our personal encounter with the text as we cross-examine it for ourselves and allow it to cross-examine us. Remember the adage: The Bible sheds a lot of light on the commentaries. All the time we should be praying for the Holy Spirit to show us the truth in our text.[8] The admonition of

Haddon Robinson at this point should be heeded: "In the approach to a passage, an interpreter must be willing to reexamine his doctrinal convictions and to reject the judgments of his most respected teachers. He must make a U-turn in his own previous understandings of the Bible should these conflict with the concept of the biblical writer."[9]

Step 3: Isolate the Dominant Truth

As we meditate on the text, a dominant thought will emerge. This dominant theme must be determined, for the whole sermon will be built around it. If you fail to discern the central thought (called the proposition by some), the sermon will probably degenerate into a lecture with many points rather than a sermon with one major thrust. So when the dominant truth is established, the next step is to express it in a clear proposition.

Step 4: Organize Your Material Around the Dominant Thought

In order to organize your material you will need the help of three things: an outline (structure), words, and illustrations.

An Outline

"The golden rule for sermon outlines is that each text must supply its own structure (outline)."[10] Thus, the number of points in a sermon should not always be three, but rather the number needed to expose the text. It is strange that our material often falls into triplets. Could it be because we are Trinitarians?[11]

I have found alliterative outlines to be effective, but only if the alliteration is true to the text and not forced. Some preachers are so intent on alliterating that they obscure the truth with their alliteration. That habit is a grievous error. It is better to be clear than to be cute.

Words

You have to clothe your thoughts in words. A preacher's words should be as simple and clear as possible. C. S. Lewis reported that he once heard a young preacher speak on the subject of repentance. He concluded his sermon with this appeal: "If you don't take seriously what I am saying, I warn you of serious eschatological consequences in the future." After the sermon, Lewis asked the preacher if he was warning his people of the risk of going to hell. "Yes," the young man replied. Lewis shot back, "Then why didn't you say so in plain English?"

Always prefer the plain, direct word to the limp, vague one. Don't "implement" promises but "keep" them. Don't say a "confrontation" but a "meeting." As my mother advised on several occasions, "Preach so third graders can understand and maybe the college folk will understand you." The language and vocabulary George Buttrick used in most of his sermons were on the seventh-grade reading level. Even his sermons preached at Harvard University were on a ninth-grade level.[12]

Profound truths can be clothed in simple words.

Illustrations

Illustrations are to a sermon what windows are to a house. They exist to shed light. The very word *illustrate* means "to throw light or lustre upon." The parables of Jesus show the importance of illustrating truth.

However, there is a danger in illustrations. The illustration can become more prominent than the truth it is intended to illuminate. Preachers are often amazed to find that people remember illustrations but miss the main point.

The best sources of illustrations are the Bible, our personal experiences, biography, and history. Printed sermons of some preachers can be a great source at times. Clarence McCartney's sermons contain excellent historical illustrations. Roy Angell's books are excellent sources of illustrations. I do not recommend sermon illustration books.

Step 5: Add the Introduction and Conclusion

First prepare the body of the sermon and then make the introduction and conclusion to fit it.

A good introduction can serve two purposes. First, it arouses interest and whets the appetite to hear the message. I have found it effective to begin my sermons with an arresting story or statement to grab the attention of the audience. Billy Graham usually begins his sermons with a pointed statement on current events. He then moves into the main thrust of the message. Also, a good introduction leads the hearer into the message itself.

An introduction should be long enough to introduce the main theme, but not so long as to detract from the sermon itself. Whether you hold your audience or not often depends upon the way you handle the introduction. Haddon Robinson solemnly declares that if the preacher does not capture attention in the first thirty seconds, he may never gain it at all.[13] Ben Haden, a Presbyterian preacher from Chattanooga, Tennessee, begins his sermons on broadcasts with several leading questions on some subject of deep interest. Then he says, "Let's talk about it." Music immediately follows, and then Mr. Haden comes back to talk about the problem. This is an example of an effective introduction on television.

Conclusions are often more difficult than introductions. Many preachers seem to be constitutionally incapable of concluding a sermon. They circle round and round like a plane on a foggy day, unable to land. A pungent definition of an optimist is that woman who slips her shoes back on in church when she hears the pastor say, "Finally." I received good advice while in seminary: "Preach the everlasting gospel, but please don't preach it everlastingly."

Conclusions should accomplish at least three purposes. First, they should recapitulate the main thrust of the sermon without re-preaching it. Second, they should make personal application of the truth. This is a very important aspect of expository preaching. Finally, they should appeal for a decision. To accomplish these three things takes all the spiritual, physical, and emotional power the preacher can muster. Preachers who extend no final invitation do no more than half the work of the preacher who does. Josh McDowell's book title is *Evidence That Demands a Verdict*. Of course it does. The preacher will never do a more important work than to persuade sinful people to obey the liberating truth he has preached. Martyn Loyd-Jones did not believe in giving an invitation for decisions at the end of the service. Swayed by hyper-

Calvinism, he thought the invitation smacked of human manipulation.[14] Certainly, the invitation can be abused and manipulated. However, the Bible abounds in many authentic invitations given by humankind and mightily used by the Holy Spirit (see Acts 2:38; Josh. 4:16). It is my conviction that people ought to have an opportunity to respond personally to the gospel immediately after it is preached, while the message is fresh and urgent, and when the Holy Spirit is calling.

The Holy Spirit is never more active than at the very moment of the invitation. Indeed, I have felt the anointing suddenly intensify during the time of the appeal. The most memorable experience I can recall was when I preached a sermon on the Mt. Carmel revival which I called "God's Answer by Fire." During the appeal I spoke these words recorded in 1 Kings 18:38: "Then the fire . . . fell." And, the very moment I spoke these words the fire indeed fell and the front filled with people professing salvation, getting right with the Lord, and praising His name. Every pastor who earnestly extends an invitation can recall such glorious moments.

Step 6: Verbalize the Message and Prepare to Deliver

There are two extremes at this point. On the one hand, some write nothing out and speak impromptu entirely. On the other hand, some write out the message in full and read the manuscript word for word. The best approach probably is to write out the message in full or to make full notes on the message. The beginning preacher is especially wise to write out his message in full, no matter how he plans to deliver it. As he becomes more experienced, he can take more liberty. Writing obliges us to study, to think straight, and to avoid old clichés. Francis Bacon was correct when he wrote, "Writing makes an exact man."

Delivering your message without notes can be very effective if you write out your material rather fully and study it thoroughly before delivery. This should not be an impossible task for the average preacher. The key is to outline your material carefully and go over it thoroughly. Robert G. Lee told me he used this method: He insisted that he did not "memorize" but rather "picturized" his prepared material. As I understand my own method, I also picturize, not memorize. I refuse to allow my mastery of the material to close out the immediate revelation and inspiration of the Holy Spirit. My choice and most valuable insights are often given to me after I enter the pulpit and while I am delivering the message. Sometimes—though not often—I have been given an entirely new message and jettisoned everything I had prepared, following the immediate promptings of the Holy Spirit.

One has to seek out God's will concerning the way he can best deliver God's message. I vividly recall how I made this a matter of prayer, asking the Lord if I should preach with or without notes. The Lord's answer seemed to be: "Prepare the best you can. Then get up and speak without notes and trust me to see you through." I have done this and the Lord has kept his promise, though a few times I was scared to death.

Later, my decision to preach without notes was encouraged by my preaching professor in seminary. Each student was required to preach two sermons for credit. I preached first from a full manuscript. Other students were reading their sermons from a manuscript, and I thought it only fair that I do the same. You can read good English much easier than you can speak it.

My professor, learning that I preached without notes in the church I served as student pastor, required me to preach my second sermon extemporaneously. Afterward, he said to me, "When I heard you preach the second time I did not recognize you as the same man I had heard before. Don't ever preach from a manuscript or notes. Preach extemporaneously." And I have followed his advice with excitement throughout my ministry.

If a preacher does not feel comfortable preaching without notes, I would suggest that the best alternative would be to reduce his material into good notes and preach from them. This seems to be the approach of most pastors today. Jonathan Edwards read from a full manuscript. Billy Graham preaches from full notes. Obviously, such men are led of God.

A Personal Testimony on Sermon Preparation

In this chapter I have discussed the successive steps the preacher may take in preparing expository sermons. At times I have followed this procedure rather closely. At other times I have greatly simplified it. I get alone with God, my Bible, and a pad of paper. I find my text. I read and re-read and re-read again. I memorize and then meditate upon it. I pore over the text until I can put it into one statement. I put a "handle" on it, with two or more points—the outline. I then develop the points with the best arguments I can muster, arguments I believe will be convincing to my audience.

Once I have given birth to my outline and thoughts, I turn to the lexicons and commentaries. I sprinkle some of their choice insights into my thoughts. But I let my own ideas be the dominant message. The finished product is basically mine. My soul overflows with joy that God has given me a message, first for my own soul and then for my people. I write out the material or put it into full notes. I then "picturize" the materials for as many hours as possible up to the time of delivery. I get into the pulpit and preach without notes. Greater joy than this has no man.

When asked how I prepare to preach I have often given the tested fourfold approach:

1. I read myself full.
2. I think myself clear.
3. I pray myself hot.
4. I get up and let go.

Let every brother find the method best for him in preparing and delivering sermons. But let no method ever become a barrier to a man hearing God's voice in his soul. Our prayer should always be that of young Samuel, "Speak, LORD, for your servant hears" (1 Sam. 3:10).

You may be asking Paul's question, "Who is sufficient for these things?" No human being who has ever lived is sufficient. Sermon preparation and delivery can only be done effectively by the grace of God and in the anointing of the Holy Spirit. If the demands of sermon preparation and delivery seem to overwhelm you, think of the high and holy calling to which our gracious God has called. Phillips Brooks once told a Yale audience, "Let us rejoice with one another that in a world where there are a great many good and happy things for men to do, God has given us the best and happiest and made us preachers of his truth."[15]

CHAPTER 9

Preparing Evangelistic Sermons

Preparing and delivering a message with the aim of making disciples for Christ is a holy task and calls forth every resource of mind and spirit that God has given us. Such sufficiency can only come from the grace of God (see 1 Cor. 15:10), but this does not exempt the preacher from observing the basic rules of effective sermon building. The most powerful evangelistic messages are generally expository in nature and follow the rules for expository preaching set forth in this book.

In addition, there are twelve practical principles which I believe are crucial in preparing and delivering evangelistic messages.

Pray It Through

The place to begin in sermon preparation is in the secret place of prayer. As we wait before the throne, we hear what God has to say about our own needs and then we can receive the message for others. This will lead us to confession, cleansing, and spiritual sensitivity. Only when our vessel is clean are we fit for the Master's use (see 2 Tim. 2:21). With a heart in tune with the will of God, we can receive God's message for the persons to whom we will be speaking and then project our thoughts to their needs. A message that hits home must meet people where they are, both in interests and attitudes, as well as in their feeling toward the preacher.

As the burden of the message and its structure take form, it should be prayed over and presented to God as an offering of devotion. Dr. Robert E. Coleman asserts, "There is a sense in which it is preached to God before anyone else. Only after the sermon has his approval can the evangelist be confident in proclaiming it to the people."[1] In my own experience I have discovered that I must first draw the sermon through my own heart or preach it to myself before I can share it with the people. I have prepared hundreds of sermons, biblical in content and expository in nature, that I never preached because my own heart never embraced them.

The spirit of prayer must persist through delivery, especially at the invitation. This communication with heaven makes the sermon "mighty in God for pulling down strongholds"

(2 Cor. 10:4). Prayer is our mightiest weapon in preaching. In his book *Master Secrets of Prayer,* C. V. Thompson quoted Sidlow Baxter as saying that men may reject everything about us— our message, our appeals, our very selves, but they are helpless against our prayers. To paraphrase the words of Dr. Lewis Sperry Chafer, "Winning souls is more a work of pleading *for* them than a service of pleading *with* them."[2]

Exalt Jesus

Jesus is the *evangel,* the Good News incarnate, "the Lamb of God who takes away the sin of the world" (John 1:29). In him every redemptive truth begins and ends. "There is no other name under heaven given among men by which we must be saved" (Acts 4:12). "He who believes in the Son has everlasting life; and he who does not believe the Son shall not see life, but the wrath of God abides on him" (John 3:36). "If anyone does not love the Lord Jesus Christ, let him be accursed" (1 Cor. 16:22). Unless people see Jesus, regardless of what else impresses them, they will not be drawn to God. "And I, if I am lifted up from the earth [on the cross, that is], will draw all peoples to Myself," said Jesus himself in John 12:32.

The revelation of God's redeeming love reaches its climax at the blood-red hill of Calvary. There, nearly two thousand years ago, Jesus bore our sins in his own body on the tree, suffering "the just for the unjust, that He might bring us to God" (1 Pet. 3:18). Though any interpretation of the Atonement falls far short of its full meaning, it is clear that Jesus was "wounded for our transgressions, He was bruised for our iniquities; the chastisement for our peace was upon Him, and by His stripes we are healed" (Isa. 53:5). Sin is a moral debt which no mortal can pay. Jesus has paid it in full, and to be saved, the lost sinner must trust in his substitutionary sacrifice in order to be forgiven and to receive the gift of his righteousness (see 2 Cor. 5:21).

The whole message, then, turns on what one does with Jesus. Keenly aware of this, the evangelist must seek to bring into focus the suffering, substitutionary love of Jesus on the cross. As Spurgeon said, "No matter what my text is, I make a beeline to the cross."

David Wilkerson points out that some charismatics in our day are guilty of preaching a "Christ-less Pentecost" when in fact Jesus Christ is the cause and the core of Pentecost. For that reason, Pentecost climaxed in the ingathering of three thousand lost souls in one day. The evangelistic message, therefore, must center in Jesus, with special emphasis on his willingness to die for each of us personally and our responsibility to accept his forgiveness by faith. As St. Augustine observed, "Jesus loved each of us, as if there were only one of us." If evangelistic preaching can press this truth to the human heart, and prove it by the sacrifice of Jesus on the cross, it will result in many being saved.

Proclaim the Scriptures

The God-breathed Word written in the book called the Bible discloses the living Word, the only Savior of humankind. As Paul declares: "All Scripture is God-breathed, and is useful for teaching, rebuking, correcting and training in righteousness, so that the man of God may be thoroughly equipped for every good work" (2 Tim. 3:16–17 NIV). The Word is the means by which the sinner knows he is lost and needs the Savior, that faith is produced in the soul (see Rom. 10:17), and that a person becomes a new creation in Christ. First Peter 1:23 says, "Having been born again, not of corruptible seed but incorruptible, through the word of God which lives and abides forever." And, "Sanctify them by Your truth. Your word is truth" (John 17:17). For this reason, the redemptive power of any sermon relates directly to the way the evangelist uses the immutable, inerrant, and life-changing Word of God (see Heb. 4:12).

The preacher's experiences and illustrations can be used to support the biblical truth, but the ultimate authority for what is preached must be the written Word of God. Experience can be trusted only when it accords with the written revelation of God in the Bible. The apostle Peter met with Jesus on the Mount of Transfiguration, but he declared that the written Word of God was a better authority than this celestial experience. "We also have the prophetic word made more sure, which you do well to heed" (2 Pet. 1:19).

Paul commissioned Timothy to "preach the Word" (2 Tim. 4:2) under all circumstances. The preacher who depends on a "Thus saith Dr. Sounding Brass" or "Dr. Dry as Dust" has violated his call, if he had one. God has spoken and the evangelist who can say, "Thus saith the Lord" will preach with authority and converting power. Such preaching needs no defense or apology. Dr. Coleman wrote of the assurance he found in the Scripture verses that promise that the Spirit of God who gave the Word will bear witness to its truthfulness (1 John 5:5; 2 Pet. 1:21) and will not let it return unto Him void (Isa. 55:11). He claimed the words gave him strength as he preached to diverse congregations, both the receptive and the "concrete" (those whose hearts seemed as hard as concrete).

As I have already related to you, there was a time when Billy Graham questioned whether the Bible was God's inerrant Word. The struggle came to a head one evening in 1949, when alone in the mountains of California, he knelt before the open Bible and said, "Here and now, by faith, I accept the Bible as thy Word. I take it all. I take it without reservations. Where there are things I cannot understand, I will reserve judgment until I receive more light. If this pleases thee, give me authority as I proclaim thy Word, and through that authority convict me of sin and turn sinners to their Savior."[3]

Within weeks, the Los Angeles Crusade started. His preaching began to manifest a new power, as he quit trying to prove the Scriptures, and simply declared, "The Bible says." To use his words, "I felt as though I were merely a voice through which the Holy Spirit was speaking."

Billy Graham discovered what every evangelist needs to know. He found that people are not interested in our ideas, nor are they moved by striking oratory. They are hungry to hear what God is saying through his Word. As Jesus said, "Man shall not live by bread alone, but by every word [rhema] that proceeds from the mouth of God" (Matt. 4:4). What God said in his inscripturated Word long ago, He still says today through his true evangelists as they preach the written Word under the anointing of the Holy Spirit. "This is a lesson every preacher must learn. And until it is reflected in our sermons, not much that we say is likely to generate faith in the hearts of hearers."[4]

136

Preach Positively

The gospel is good news. But much that has been called gospel preaching has been "bad" rather than good news. Much so-called gospel preaching is a set of "don'ts." The gospel is not a recitation of what men should not do; the gospel is not even about what men should do. The gospel is the good news of what God has done, is doing, and can do through Jesus Christ. I used to live next door to a humble Christian lady who literally "raved" about how her pastor preached the gospel. When I asked her to share some highlights of his messages, she always replied with words like this: "Our preacher really preached a red-hot sermon against TV today." "The pastor said people who smoke, drink, and go to movies are going to hell." This dear lady thought her pastor was preaching the gospel, but he was doing the very opposite. He was proclaiming the "bad" news.

Dr. Ralph Herring, for twenty-five years the pastor of First Baptist Church in Winston-Salem, North Carolina, spoke profound words I shall never forget. He said, "A person is neither saved nor sanctified by what he gives up, but by what he receives." I believe many remain lost because they are obsessed with what they must give up rather than what they receive in salvation. Never once have I regretted one thing I had to give up. So great are the positive benefits of salvation that anything I or anyone has ever given up is but rubbish compared to the "excellence of the knowledge of Christ Jesus my Lord" (Phil. 3:8). This the evangelist must believe, experience, and proclaim to be an effective communicator to lost humanity.

Personalize Sin

Humankind cannot be saved until they know they are lost; and they cannot know they are lost until they know they are sinners. Not only must they know they are sinners, but that they are lost sinners hastening to hell without Jesus Christ. Dr. Coleman says the sinner must be awakened in his conscience to see "the greatness of his guilt" and "the imminence of his doom."[5]

The diverse kinds of sin cannot be treated in one sermon. However, the basic issues of rebellion, self-righteousness, unbelief, and actual transgressions can be disclosed, with perhaps a few specific applications to the local situation. Above all, the evangelist must show the lost person that the ultimate expression of sin comes in his defiant rejection of Jesus Christ. Jesus said that when the Holy Spirit is come, he will convict and convince the world "of sin ... because they do not believe in Me" (John 16:8-9). "He who does not believe is condemned already, because he has not believed in the name of the only begotten Son of God" (John 3:18).

The evangelist should always pray for special wisdom to confront hypocrites, false professors, and lost church members of their need to repent and be saved. Satan's foremost delight is to send a person directly from the pew into hell. Dr. James Kennedy says that a high percentage of Presbyterians have never truly trusted Christ. Many of his members, he says, in the Coral Ridge Church in Ft. Lauderdale are converted church members. When someone asked him if he was not afraid of robbing people of their assurance of salvation, he replied, "You can't unseat the elect." I have never found a palatable way of preaching against sin. While, of course, considerations of propriety and good taste must be kept in mind, a sermon must get under a person's skin and make him squirm under conviction of sin.[6]

Moreover, there should never be any confusion about whom the evangelist is addressing. The preacher should talk about sin in practice, not sin in theory. Indeed, it might well seem to the sinner that the preacher has been following him around all week, noting every wrong deed and thought. One morning after I had preached against sin, one lady commented at the door, "Pastor, you have been reading my mail this week." One of the truly convincing evidences that God leads his preachers is the way he enables them to draw a picture of people in his audience of whom he knows little or nothing.

A message that does not deal with sin—the cause of all human woe—is irrelevant to human need. Though the tragedy of rebellion and its results may be bad news, still the gospel shines through, for God judges that he might save. The fact is a person can never appreciate the good news until he has first heard the bad news. John Wesley said, "I can never preach grace until I have first preached law." One thing is certain: If people do not recognize their problem, they will not want the cure. After the evangelist has preached, the lost should be crying out as did the Philippian jailer, "What must I do to be saved" from my sins which are wrecking my life and will ultimately send me to eternal hell? (see Acts 16:30–31). Whether the sinner responds in this way or not depends greatly on the way the preacher confronts him with his sin.

Keep the Sermon Comparatively Brief

There is no instruction in Scripture as to the length of a sermon. But it stands to reason that a message addressed to those without Christ should be shorter than those spoken to the children of light. God's children love the Word. As it is preached in power, their spirits are quickened and their hearts are made happy in being reminded of their riches in Christ Jesus. But the lost man, the natural man, is devoid of the Holy Spirit and does not receive the things of the Spirit of God because they are spiritually discerned (see 1 Cor. 2:14). Realizing this truth, the evangelist is wise to focus on the problems of the lost, the provision of the Savior, and the need for personal response within a brief enough time as not to lose the interest or attention of those in darkness.

This appeal should be followed by an invitation which should not be too brief or too long. Who can know the correct length of an invitation? Only the Holy Spirit, so the evangelist must depend on him with all his soul as he makes his appeal to the souls of men. We who believe in seeing people saved should always be prepared for an extended invitation. When the Holy Spirit is moving, he will often extend the invitation because of his love for those for whom Jesus died (see Rom. 15:30). For this reason, the message preceding the invitation, under most circumstances, should be relatively brief. In the final analysis, the length of an evangelistic service should be determined by the leading of the Holy Spirit.

In my own heart, I have felt the definite leading of the Holy Spirit to make the message relatively brief, but to be prepared to cast aside every preconceived idea and follow the Holy Spirit. It is interesting to note that the most successful evangelist in the twentieth century,

Billy Graham, preaches messages of about twenty-five to thirty minutes and gives an invitation for a relatively brief time.

Stick to the Point

"He took a text, he departed therefrom, and he never returned." I'm afraid this could be the epitaph on many evangelists' tombstones. But such an approach is devastating to evangelistic endeavor. The preacher should ask himself, "What is it I want to get across?" Unless the evangelist knows what he is aiming for, almost no one else will catch on. My homiletics professor warned me against uncertainty in the pulpit with the words, "A fog in the pulpit will produce darkness in the pew."

To avoid rambling and to stay on course, I recommend these simple procedures:

1. Write out your objective in one sentence.
2. Work out a simple, balanced outline.
3. Let your points flow effortlessly out of the passage.
4. Develop a progression of thought leading up to the appeal.
5. Use some concrete, down-to-earth illustrations, drawn from your own life. Make them relatively brief. People like stories, but do not let your stories

overshadow God's truth. More important is the logic of the truth presented.
6. Study much. Don't rely on "warmed over" material.

Wise counsel was given by John Wesley when he told his preachers, "Take care not to ramble, but keep to the text, and make out what you take in hand."[7]

Make It Simple

Paul declares, "But even if our gospel is veiled, it is veiled to those who are perishing" (2 Cor. 4:3). There is one sure way to hide our message from those who need it most; namely, couch it in language not understood by the hearers. Dr. Robert Coleman has written a scathing indictment of abstruse preaching. He says,

A well-prepared sermon will be uncomplicated in its basic organization and language (see 2 Cor. 11:3). Truth when reduced to its highest expression is always simple. Anybody can make the Gospel difficult to comprehend, but the person of wisdom says it so that a child can understand. Some preachers feign intellectual superiority by sermonizing in high-sounding philosophic terms, as if the message needed to be sophisticated in order to appeal to the well-educated. That some clerics labor under this illusion may explain why so many people, including university students, scorn the church. Whenever a theological discourse gets so complicated that only a college-educated person can understand it, then something is wrong, either with the theology or with its presentation.[8]

Paul, the most astute theologian in the history of the church, was probably the simplest in his language. "My speech and my preaching were not with persuasive words of human wisdom, but in demonstration of the Spirit and of power, that your faith should not be in the wisdom of men but in the power of God" (1 Cor. 2:4–5).

When the gospel of salvation is stated plainly as a fact and illustrated concretely, it makes sense to the honest soul seeking after God. Before I preach I try to visualize the person who is uneducated and whose understanding is very limited. Then I endeavor to put my message in words this person can understand. I have discovered that profound truths can be expressed in simple language. Also I have made it a rule never to preach on any subject which I had not grasped myself. Even though I have wanted to preach on certain subjects, if I did not understand to my heart's satisfaction, I postponed preaching until my mind had comprehended it. For this reason, I preached very little on prophecy the first twenty years of my ministry. I weary of young evangelists who speak so eloquently and confidently on themes they do not comprehend themselves and yet pose as having the last word. Such prideful showmanship has hurt the cause of evangelism immensely.

Because of my humble beginnings and the counsel of my wise and godly mother, I have always endeavored to preach in the simplest language I know. The reaction of my audiences has been most rewarding. One brother, with little education, started visiting our worship services. As he would leave the services, he would say to me Sunday after Sunday, "Bill, you are the only preacher I ever heard who could keep my mind out of the cornfield. For the first time I am understanding what the Bible says." A few months later this humble man received Christ as his Savior and Lord. Of all the people I have ever been instrumental in winning to Christ, this man exuded the most joy and appreciation. His name was John, and I nicknamed him "Joy John." I named his right foot "Glory" and his left foot "Hallelujah," so when he walked he would be saying, "Glory, hallelujah!"

The purpose of education for the preacher is to give him the ability not only to understand theological truth, but to be able to communicate it in simple language. The most encouraging compliment I ever remember was given by an honest Sunday school teacher. In her visitation one evening, she encountered a lady who had a deadly horror of an educated ministry. Her denomination had taught her that education for a preacher was of the devil. She asked this teacher the question, "Is your pastor educated?" To which the teacher replied, "Yes, he is, but you would never know it, so come on to church." In my judgment, this is the way God would have it for his evangelistic preacher—be educated but do not flaunt it. Preach simply, so simple people can hear the simple gospel and simply be saved.

Make the Message Urgent

No evangelist should ever preach in a "take-it-or-leave-it" manner. The lack of urgency is the one unpardonable sin in evangelistic preaching. If that note is lacking, nothing else can make up for it. There is an absolute necessity of urgency when speaking to human beings under "the sentence of death." The following episode vividly illustrates this truth:

A preacher was invited to address the inmates of a large penitentiary. The afternoon before he was to speak he paid a visit to the institution. The warden showed him around, and at last they came to the chapel. It was a large auditorium seating about fifteen hundred people. "It will be full tomorrow morning, sir," said the officer. It was not the number of seats, but rather the two particular seats on the front

146

row that intrigued the preacher. "Why are these two chairs here in front draped in black?" he asked. The warden replied, "The two men who will occupy those seats tomorrow are under sentence of death. On Monday they go to the electric chair!" "Under sentence of death," repeated the minister quietly. And then he said, "Do I understand that this will be the last service they will ever attend?" "Yes, sir," was the reply. "Your sermon will be the last one they will ever hear."

The preacher had seen all he wanted to. He must find a place to be alone and do some quiet thinking. When he reached home, he went to his study, took out the sermon he had prepared, reviewed it, then tore it up! "This is of no use," he said. "It does not meet the need." Then falling on his knees, he prayed, "O God, give me a message for those two men who will be sitting in those draped chairs."[9]

There are "draped chairs" in every congregation; therefore, the preacher must preach with a sense of urgency.[10] One does not have to be loud to be urgent. But one must be moved to the depths of his soul over the lostness of humankind and to plead in Christ's stead that they be reconciled to God (see 2 Cor. 5:20).

Press for a Verdict

One avid fisherman was asked after a fishing adventure, "Did you catch any fish?" He replied, "No, but we surely did influence a lot of trout." Our job is not just to influence human-kind. Our task is to call them to make a decisive verdict for Christ.

Much preaching today expects no decisions and therefore gets none. If the world would call us arrogant in pleading for a verdict, let them be reminded that Joshua called on people to choose "this day" (see Josh. 24:15). Paul warned people that time is running out, "Behold, now is the accepted time; behold, now is the day of salvation" (2 Cor. 6:2). The writer of Hebrews said three times in succession, "Today if you will hear His voice, do not harden your hearts" (3:7–8, 15; 4:7). Jesus called for a verdict on many occasions (see Matt. 11:28, Luke 19:5, and others). He commanded Zaccheus to descend from the tree where he was perched with urgent words, "Zaccheus, make haste and come down, for today I must stay at your house" (Luke 19:5).

Dr. Robert Coleman writes,

> The decision is what makes the difference; if the will is not moved to action, there can be no salvation (Rom. 10:13). The truth of the message, thus, is saved from degenerating into mere rationalism on the one hand and mere emotionalism on the other by linking it with a personal response. To stir people to great aspirations without also giving them something that they can do about it leaves them worse off than they were before. They will

likely become either more confused in their thinking, or more indifferent in their will. Consequently, once the Gospel is made clear, the evangelist must call to account each person who hears the message. So far as he knows, this may be their last opportunity to respond.[11]

A man once said to Dr. R. A. Torrey, "I'm not a Christian, but I am moral and upright. I would like to know what you have against me." Torrey looked the man in the eye and replied, "I charge you, sir, with treason against heaven's king."[12]

This is the issue which must be faced. Therefore, the evangelist must seek "to persuade men" to come to a verdict. The evangelist cannot make the decision for anyone; but, as God leads, he is responsible for doing what he can to make the issues clear. I call revivals "Eternity Week," because eternal destinies are at stake. The effective evangelist will pray, persuade, and plead for a verdict since this is true.

Plead for Souls

People should never be manipulated; it is abominable to trick them into making decisions. But the souls of men are worth pleading for. Paul pleads for the souls of men and urges all Christians to do the same. "We implore you on Christ's behalf, be reconciled to God"

(2 Cor. 5:20). Pleading, of course, should precede our preaching. It should take place in prayer as we prepare and as we visualize those who need to be saved. But it should also take place in the pulpit with a tenderness that the hearer is quick to recognize. One of the finest definitions I ever heard of evangelism is this: "Evangelism is one beggar telling another beggar where to find bread." If we have partaken of the bread, our own soul has been satisfied. Then with brokenness and empathy, we can yearn that people might come and eat of the same bread and drink freely from the same fountain of living water. A satisfied customer is the best advertisement.

A few years after the death of the famous Scottish preacher Robert Murray McCheyne, a young minister visited his church to discover the secret of the man's amazing influence. The sexton, who had served under McCheyne, took the youthful inquirer into the vestry, and asked him to sit in the chair used by the former pastor.

"Now put your elbows on the table," he said, "Now put your face in your hands." The visitor obeyed. "Now let the tears flow! "That was the way Mr. McCheyne used to do!"[13]

Yes, that is the way to do it. Plead for souls. In order to do so, the evangelist must feel the weight of their lostness, knowing their destiny may hang upon his one sermon preached on that one occasion.

Depend on the Holy Spirit

Apart from the power of the Holy Spirit, everything said thus far would be sounding brass and a tinkling cymbol. The indispensable place of the Holy Spirit in sermon preparation and delivery is dealt with in chapter 12. However, I especially feel it is necessary to show the specific role of the Holy Spirit in evangelistic preaching. Jesus Himself said the Holy Spirit is the Great Evangelizer, convicting and convincing the world of sin, righteousness and judgment (John 16:8–11). This being true, the evangelistic preacher must be the channel through which the Holy Spirit exerts his power to the lost world. This means the evangelist must be born of the Holy Spirit, but also filled, led, and controlled by the Holy Spirit. When the people hear the evangelist, they should hear two voices, the voice of the preacher from the pulpit and also the voice of the Holy Spirit in the soul. When these two voices agree, the miracle of salvation begins to take place.

Dr. Robert Coleman is one of the most powerful evangelists of our day, not because of his intellect (though it is great), but because of his experience of the Holy Spirit. Listen to his words as he writes about the Holy Spirit and evangelism:

> The third Person of the Trinity effects in and through us what Christ has done for us. It is the Spirit who gives life; the flesh profits nothing (see John 6:63). He initiates and guides prayer. He lifts up the Son, thereby drawing persons to the Father. He makes the inspired Scripture come alive. He convicts of sin, of righteousness, and of judgment. He guides the obedient servant into truth, making the message clear to seeking hearts. He recreates and sanctifies through the Word. And He extends the call for weary and heavy laden souls to come to Jesus. From beginning to end, the whole enterprise of evangelism is in the authority and demonstration of God's Spirit.
>
> We can understand, then, why the glorified Savior told His disciples to tarry until they be filled with His Spirit (see Luke 24:49; Acts 1:4, 5, 8). How else could they fulfill their mission? The Word and work of their Lord had to become a burning compulsion within them. The superhuman ministry to which they were called required supernatural help—an enduement of power from on high.
>
> This is nowhere more necessary than with Gospel preachers. Any sermon that circumvents this provision will be as lifeless as it is barren. So let us trust Him. As God has called us into His harvest, He will provide what is needed to do the work. The secret of

evangelism, finally, is to let the Holy Spirit have His way.[14]

The highest and happiest call upon humankind is the divine call to preach the gospel of God's redeeming love in Christ. The most effective method of proclaiming this glorious message is through expository preaching. The finest expression of expository preaching is evangelistic proclamation. I do not have the words to express my enthusiasm for and recommendation of expository preaching, especially when its aim is the winning of disciples to Christ. With Isaiah and Paul I declare, "How beautiful are the feet of those who preach the gospel of peace, who bring glad tidings of good things!" (Isa. 52:7; Rom. 10:15).

153

CHAPTER 10

Methods of Sermon Delivery

Effective delivery is as important as effective preparation. Four common methods of sermon delivery are the manuscript method, memory method, impromptu method, and the extemporaneous method. Each offers strengths and weaknesses for the preacher.

The Manuscript Method

In the manuscript method the sermon is written out in full, and the preacher reads it word for word. This method assures that no part of the message will be forgotten and enables the preacher to choose carefully his words and vocabulary.

However, the disadvantages of this method

outweigh the advantages. Reading a sermon tends to be dead and monotonous. Few preachers can read a sermon effectively. What of Jonathan Edwards, who preached his famous sermon "Sinners in the Hands of an Angry God" (and others) from a manuscript? Edwards is the exception to the rule. Jerry Vines is correct when he says, "Rare is the preacher who can read so well that the sermon seems to be coming from the heart as well as his head."[1]

Did you hear about the preacher who was reading his manuscript when a puff of wind blew the sermon off the pulpit into the yard outside? A milk cow came along and ate the manuscript. She dried up.

The Memory Method

When this method is used, the sermon is written out in full, committed to memory, and then delivered without any manuscript or notes. Such a sermon might be impressive, but memorized messages sound canned and even superficial. The preacher may appear to be acting more than preaching. Concentrating on remembering may cause the preacher to ignore the Holy Spirit's revealing new thoughts during the midst of the sermon. The danger also is that the preacher may forget part of his sermon.

The Impromptu Method

With the impromptu method, no prior preparation is made. The preacher speaks "off the top of his head." I will not say that the Sovereign God could never enable one to preach like this. But this method is not condoned in the Word of God and has nothing to commend it to the serious preacher of the Word of God.

The Extemporaneous Method

In the extemporaneous approach the preacher prepares carefully. He may make copious notes and may even write out a full manuscript. He studies his material carefully and diligently. He delivers the message in his own words, with the actual wording of the sermon being left to the moment of delivery.

The advantages of this method are that the preacher is free in his delivery and has constant eye contact with his audience. Moreover, great freshness in expression is possible. The Holy Spirit is free to speak to the preacher on the spot.

Some disadvantages exist with the extemporaneous method. The preacher may find himself using the same words and phrases over and over. He also faces the danger of rambling. When the preacher relies too heavily upon his ability to speak extemporaneously, he may relax his habits of study. When this happens, a sermon delivered extemporaneously becomes terribly bad. One poor extemporaneous sermon can bring discredit to the expository method of sermon preparation.[2] Done well, the extemporaneous method of delivery can be the most effective.

Many of the expositors through the centuries have employed the extemporaneous method in delivery. This was the method of Alexander Maclaren and G. Campbell Morgan, both considered to be expositors *par excellence*.[3]

Many of the effective preachers of our day use this method. It is the method of Stephen Olford, W. A. Criswell, Leo Eddleman, Jerry Vines, Adrian Rogers, among others. The method of Robert G. Lee is difficult to classify. In the latter years of his life, he told me that he did not memorize his sermons but "picturized" the main points in his messages. He probably combined the memory and extemporaneous methods. Whatever his method, his preaching impressed the hearer as the very best in extemporaneous preaching.

The methods of delivery are extremely important in the art of proclamation. However, the way the message comes across to the listener also depends greatly on the style of delivery. One's diction, elocution, emotion, "body language," pathos, even one's dress, are powerful ingredients in communicating the gospel.

Consideration of these factors would be a major study in themselves, and they do not fall within the scope of this book. For example, the pathos in Dr. George Truett's voice would be a major study within itself. The most vital, single ingredient in delivery is what W. E. Sangster calls the "plus" of the Holy Spirit—that special touch for the special task, the "anointing." I deal with this vital subject in chapter 12.

CHAPTER 11

Some Dangers to Avoid

Paul says we have the treasure of the gospel in earthen vessels (see 2 Cor. 4:7). This is painfully true, and any preacher who denies his human weaknesses makes a mistake. On the other hand, a more serious mistake is to let our human weaknesses or strengths hinder the message of the glorious gospel.

We should not permit "ourselves" to spoil the effectiveness of our preaching; ego is the greatest enemy of the preacher. Dr. Loyd-Jones aptly declares, "And the only way to deal with self is to be so taken up with . . . the glory of what we are doing that we forget ourselves altogether."[1] Few can forget themselves altogether; we can, however, watch ourselves, and, by the grace of God, watch ourselves very carefully. We need to avoid certain dangers like a plague.

Professionalism

Probably the greatest of all dangers in the ministry is professionalism. The "professional" is the preacher who preaches because it is expected. Proclamation of the gospel has become only a job. Preaching has become routine, like acting a part. Preachers have to fight against this as long as they live.

One friend candidly admitted to me, "The only reason I preach is because 11:00 A.M. rolls around every Sunday." This brother was suffering from burnout. He called it, rightly, "spiritual shell shock." Many there are who preach for no other reason than that they are expected to do so at the appointed hour. Here is my formula to avoid burnout: Stay on your knees and in the Word, depend constantly upon the Holy Spirit, sleep adequately, exercise regularly, stay close to your people, and go soul-winning weekly.

Display of Knowledge

A good preacher has knowledge and is accumulating more all the time. But to parade it and display it are bad in every sense. A great theologian once said, "No preacher can preach Christ and him crucified and at the same time give the impression that he is clever." I have observed that the preacher most inclined to display his learning is usually relatively uneducated. Whatever our learning, it should all be placed at the feet of Jesus to be used for his glory. Dr. Leo Eddleman used to say to me, "Everybody ought to get enough education that no one will look down on him, and if God leads, he should go on and get enough education that he will not look down on anybody else."

In the beginning years of my ministry I could hardly wait for the music to stop, so I could deliver the "masterpiece" I had prepared. I soon learned that such an attitude was a trap from Satan. Rather than resting proudly in my preparation, I learned to approach the pulpit "in fear and trembling." I am still haunted by a sermon delivered on Easter Sunday, 1952, based on 2 Corinthians 5:1, "For we know that if our earthly house, this tent, is destroyed, we have a building from God, a house not made with hands, eternal in the heavens." I started out well but soon lost power. I never regained it, and the sermon fell to the ground. Dr. Robert G. Lee would have said that I "laid the foundation for a skyscraper and proceeded to build a chicken coop on top of it." Paul would have said, "Let him who thinks he stands take heed lest he fall" (1 Cor. 10:12).

Relying on a Good Voice

God has gifted many preachers with good voices. But the preacher should neither rely on or flaunt this natural ability. Martyn Loyd-Jones gives this warning:

> Watch your natural gifts. . . . Watch your strength, not so much weakness. It is your strength you have to watch, the things at which you excel, your natural gifts and aptitudes. They are the ones most likely to trip you because they are the ones that will tempt you to make a display or to pander to self. So watch these and also your idiosyncrasies." [2]

Being a Character

Some preachers have certain traits that make them characters—some things out of the ordinary that make them cute or attractive. It may be their voices, looks, mannerisms, humor, or wardrobes. The danger is to play up the unusual and call attention to oneself. Of course, if you are naturally a character and don't play up to it, the Holy Spirit can use your uniqueness in getting out God's message. Dr. Vance Havner was a good example of this. He had a country drawl (he was reared in the mountains of North Carolina) and a dry sense of humor. Both were natural parts of his personality. The Lord used these traits to great effect in Havner's preaching. Dr. Angel Martinez, the evangelist, is another preacher whose natural traits are used by God. Angel's penetrating (Spanish) accent and his appearance electrify audiences all over the nation.

Pride

St. Augustine said that pride is the deadliest of all sins (see Prov. 16:18), and pride is never more deadly than in the preacher. Pride assumes many forms. The preacher should know this and fight against it at all times. The best way of checking pride is to keep our eyes on Christ crucified. Isaac Watts expressed this truth in his great hymn:

> *When I survey the wondrous cross,*
> *On which the Prince of Glory died,*
> *My richest gain I count but loss*
> *And pour contempt on all my pride.*

A sure antidote, according to Dr. Loyd-Jones is "to read on Sunday nights the biography of some great saint," such as George Whitefield or David Brainerd.[3]

Browbeating

Some preaching is all "demand" and no exposition of the truth. The preacher spends the whole sermon "getting at" the people rather than teaching them. Some proscriptions are needed, but too much exhortation is counterproductive.

Polemics

The Scriptures have a pronounced polemical element at some points, and so must our preaching; we have to warn and guide our people. But you must not assume the role of defender of the truth and spend your time arguing viewpoints and attacking people. No life is in such words, and this approach will certainly ruin the life of your church.

A number of great preachers have done great damage to their people by feeding them a steady diet of the proofs of biblical inerrancy. One brother reprimanded me for not preaching more on this subject. I replied, "God did not call me to defend the Bible but to proclaim it." I am not saying that we should never preach on biblical inerrancy and that I consider the doctrine unimportant. I am saying that we should not ride that doctrine or any other as a hobby horse.

On the other hand, we must not fall into the error of always being positive. "Never negative, always positive" is humbug, hypocrisy.[4] Vance Havner said we could preach in the positives all the time if we wanted to, but we needed to understand that while we were preaching in the positives, our people were living in the negatives.

Irony

Many people take you literally and are thus offended by irony. Be very careful with it. Anything that smacks of sarcasm or the belittling of others has no place in the pulpit. To belittle people, you have to be little.

Familiarity

By familiarity, I mean a forced folksyness in the pulpit. The preacher who goes into the pulpit with a contrived smile and greets the congregation with the words, "Hi folks, nice to see you. How good of you to come," and then cracks a joke or two to put people at ease, may be falling into this trap. There is a place for sanctified humor in the pulpit, especially the kind so masterfully used by Robert G. Lee and Vance Havner. But a constant joke just to be entertaining is degrading in a service intended to glorify the triune God. Humor and being down-to-earth, when they come naturally and arise without any strained effort, can be of great value to the preacher.

Imitation

To mimic another's voice in order to appear pious or spiritual is a serious mistake. It is a sign of weakness and immaturity and is not appreciated by the people. God has given us natural voices which are beautiful to him and quite acceptable to the people when we use them naturally.

Some preachers have tried to imitate Billy Graham. I know a man, very promising and far above average in ability, who almost ruined his preaching by obviously trying to sound like Billy Graham. I am happy to say that he later saw his error, became himself, and has become a good preacher and teacher. Another friend, at an early age, began to copy the style of W. A. Criswell and use his gestures. He has never had the wisdom to change. I say to my people, "I can't be a George Truett or a W. A. Criswell, but I'm the best specimen of Bill Bennett the world has ever seen." Each of us is "fearfully and wonderfully made" (Ps. 139:14). We should be satisfied to be who we are.

I urge every preacher to be natural. God made you unique. He will use you gloriously to preach his Word if you will be yourself and let the Holy Spirit use your natural abilities. Warren Wiersbe counseled preachers to know, accept, and develop themselves, and to learn from other preachers rather than mimic or imitate them.

Excessive Talking About Yourself and Family

An egotist is a person who talks so much about himself that you don't have any time to talk about yourself. The point is that no one wants to hear you talk too much about yourself and family. Some sharing is in order at appropriate times, but too much is highly offensive. I know a compassionate and strong Bible preacher who often ruins his excellent sermons by praising his wife. I do not want to be misunderstood. I believe the preacher, and especially the pastor of a church, should show the highest respect and love for his wife and children from the pulpit, and in order to do so he must allude to them from time to time. Just do not overdo it.

Criticizing Other Preachers

Obviously all preachers do not agree with one another. But the pulpit is no place to express criticism against a fellow pastor. To run down another preacher from the pulpit is an abomination. A man who has to tear down others to build himself up is a little man. One of the most visible, successful pastors in America recently wrote an article entitled "If I Had My Ministry to Do Over Again, What Would I Do Differently?" This powerful leader wrote, "I would never speak a word against another man of God."

Opening with an Apology

A sermon should not be opened with an apology. A congregation will not be persuaded by such a preacher.[5]

Let me call your attention to a statement made by Dr. Russell Dicks, an authority on pastoral care. He gave this advice to his students. "You have a great opportunity to do much good in your ministry if you don't do too much wrong." This is a statement every preacher should remember. By God's enabling grace, avoid doing those things which hinder people from hearing the glorious message God has given you to preach.

CHAPTER 12

In the Power of the Spirit

The Spiritual Factor
in Sermon Delivery

The greatest single need in the modern pulpit is the anointing of the Holy Spirit, which enables mere men to preach in supernatural power. If the anointing is lacking, no mastery of methods can make up for its absence. The preacher may hold college and seminary degrees. He may have an earned doctorate in theology. His sermons may be homiletical masterpieces. His delivery may be flawless. He may have a charismatic personality. But without the unction of the Holy Spirit, his sermons will not be effective.

Careful preparation and unction of the Holy Spirit are not contrary to each other but complementary. In fact, Martyn Loyd-Jones suggests that the way to look upon the unction of the Spirit is to think of it as that which comes upon the preparation. There is a close affinity between the work of the Holy Spirit and a trained mind. An incident in the Old Testament proves this relationship. Elijah faced the false prophets of Israel on Mount Carmel. Elijah first built an altar; next he cut wood and put it on the altar; then, he killed a bullock, cut it in pieces, and put the pieces on the wood. Finally, having done all that, he prayed, and the fire fell (see 1 Kings 18:20–38). That is the divine order. As Haddon Robinson so beautifully expressed it, "True preaching comes when the loving heart and disciplined mind are laid at the disposal of the Holy Spirit."[1]

The gospel preacher has a definite advantage over all other public communicators. This advantage is the anointing of the Holy Spirit which enables the preacher to be sharp, persuasive, and productive. This ingredient distinguishes gospel preaching from all other methods of communication.[2]

The New Testament refers often to anointed preaching. Jesus spoke of His own anointing to preach in these words,

The Spirit of the LORD is upon Me, because He has anointed Me to preach the gospel to the poor . . . to heal the brokenhearted, to preach deliverance to the captives and recovery of sight to the blind, to set at liberty those who are oppressed, to preach the acceptable year of the LORD (Luke 4:18–19).

Acts 10:38 declares that "God anointed Jesus of Nazareth with the Holy Spirit and with power, who went about doing good and healing all who were oppressed of the devil, for God was with Him." John R. Rice, in his book about the Holy Spirit, stressed that Jesus never preached a sermon, never won a soul, and never performed an act of healing until He was anointed with the Holy Spirit. He then added, "If Jesus, the Son of God, needed the anointing for ministry during the days of His flesh, how much more do we need it?" Martyn Loyd-Jones likewise asserted that even our Lord Himself, the Son of God, could not have exercised His ministry as a man on earth if He had not received this special, peculiar anointing of the Holy Spirit.[3]

The apostle Paul was superbly educated and trained in speaking. But he made it crystal clear to the Corinthians that he came not "with excellence of speech or of wisdom declaring . . . the testimony of God" (1 Cor. 2:1). "And my speech," Paul continued, "and my preaching were not with persuasive words of human wisdom, but in demonstration of the Spirit and of power" (1 Cor. 2:4). Paul did not depend upon Greek rhetoric, so honored in Corinth, but on the anointing power of the Holy Spirit. Consequently, Paul could testify that miraculous things happened when he preached; people were saved, healed, and delivered from demons. The Corinthian speakers were noted for their oratorical abilities. Their listeners were spellbound, but no souls were saved, and no lives were changed. Likewise today, the preacher may impress his listeners with powerful rhetoric and psychological skills but actually leave them unmoved at the deepest level of their existence.[4] Preaching, to be effective, must be more than eloquent words; it must be in the demonstration of the Holy Spirit's power. Such preaching produces transforming and eternal results which no one can deny.

I know of no preacher personally, nor have I ever read of one, who was mightily used by God, yet was not anointed with the Holy Spirit. Oswald Chambers was filled with the Holy Spirit when he heard F. B. Meyer preach on the infilling. The next time Chambers preached, the people flocked to the front during the invitation, making decisions for Christ. Chambers was overwhelmed at the power of his message and cried out, "Lord, what has happened?" The Lord answered, "Chambers, didn't you ask me to fill you?"

One day D. L. Moody was filled with the Holy Spirit on the streets of New York City. So mighty was the surge of God's love in his soul that he asked God to stay his hand. After his infilling, Moody continued to preach his same sermons but with a new freshness, vitality, and effectiveness. Moody said, "You can breathe without lungs, see without eyes, and hear without ears as quickly as you can live the Christian life without the infilling of the Holy Spirit." *etc.*

The world still marvels at the ministry of Charles H. Spurgeon in the nineteenth century. Five thousand people turned out to hear him on Sunday mornings. Five thousand people more heard him on Sunday evenings, as he preached the unsearchable riches of Christ in the power of the Holy Spirit. Fifteen steps led up to the pulpit of the Metropolitan Tabernacle in London. It is said that as Spurgeon mounted those stairs with slow, methodical steps, he muttered at each step, "I believe in the Holy Ghost."[5] Paul Yonggi Cho, pastor of the world's largest church, calls the Holy Spirit his "Senior Partner."

In his excellent book on the Holy Spirit, Billy Graham describes the crisis which led to his being filled or anointed with the Holy Spirit. Here are Billy's own words:

We sailed for England in 1954 for a crusade that was to last for three months. While on ship I experienced a definite sense of oppression. Satan seemed to have assembled a formidable array of his artillery against me.

Not only was I oppressed, I was overtaken by a sense of depression accompanied by a frightening feeling of inadequacy for the task that lay ahead. Almost night and day I prayed. . . . Then one day in a prayer meeting with my wife and colleagues, a break came. As I wept before the Lord I was filled with a deep assurance that power belonged to God and He was faithful. I had been baptized into the body of Christ when I was saved, but I believe God gave me a special anointing on the way to England. From that moment on, I was confident that God the Holy Spirit was in control for the task of the 1954 Crusade in London. Experiences of this kind had happened to me before and they have happened to me many times since. Sometimes no tears are shed. Sometimes as I have lain awake at night the quiet assurance has come that I was being filled with the Holy Spirit for the task that lay ahead. . . . There have been many more occasions which I would have to say as the apostle Paul did in 1 Corinthians 2:3, "I was with you in weakness, in fear and in much trembling."[6]

The Anointing

The question arises, "What is the anointing of the Holy Spirit?" Let the Scriptures speak at this point. Already we have noted Paul's word that the anointing is the "demonstration of the Spirit and of power" in the preaching

174

of the Word (see 1 Cor. 2:4). Again Paul gives a precise definition of the anointing in 1 Thessalonians 1:5, "For our gospel did not come to you in word only, but also in power, and in the Holy Spirit and in much assurance." The apostle Peter describes the anointing as preaching "the gospel to you by the Holy Spirit sent from heaven" (1 Pet. 1:12).

Anointed men through the ages have described the anointing upon them in various ways. Charles G. Finney described the anointing as "rivers of liquid love" flowing through him. Billy Graham described his anointing as a "deep assurance that power belonged to God, that he was faithful, and in control." Martyn Loyd-Jones, who believed the anointing was "the greatest essential . . . in preaching," defined the anointing in these words:

> It is the Holy Spirit falling upon the preacher in a special manner. It is an access of power. It is God giving power, and enablement, through the Spirit, to the preacher in order that he may do his work in a manner that lifts it up beyond the efforts and endeavors of man to a position in which the preacher is being used by the Spirit and becomes the channel through which the Spirit works. This is seen very plainly and clearly in the Scriptures.[7]

Loyd-Jones goes on to describe the actual feeling of the anointed preacher, no doubt giving his own experience:

M.
Lloyd Jones
describes
the
anointing

I know of nothing on earth that is comparable to this feeling. . . . When this happens you have a feeling that you are not actually doing the preaching. You are looking on. It is not your effort; you are just the instrument, the channel, the vehicle; and the Spirit is using you and you are looking on in great enjoyment and astonishment. There is nothing that is in any way comparable to this.[8]

I heard of a church in which a certain deacon often prayed publicly, "Lord, please unctionize our pastor." After hearing this prayer several times, the pastor asked the deacon one day, "What do you mean by unction?" The deacon replied, "I don't know what it is; but whatever it is, I know you ain't got it." To define the anointing is not easy. One thing is clear: When the anointing is present, people know it; when it is absent, they also know it.

A Heart Preacher

Someone has said, "A message prepared in the head will reach the head; but a message prepared in the heart will reach the heart." We need preaching that will reach the hearts of people in our day. We are literally cursed by too much heartless and tearless preaching. We have lost our capacity to weep. We have become so professional and intellectual that we have lost our deep feeling. This is not an

176

affliction of liberal preachers only. Conservatives suffer from the same malady. Not only are we threatened by an unbelieving liberalism in many circles, but by a dead, heartless orthodoxy. Vance Havner said, "You can be as theologically straight as a gun barrel and as spiritually empty." A tearless, heartless preacher will not move modern man. Samuel May said to Lloyd Garrison, "Oh my friend, try to be more cool; you are all on fire." Garrison replied, "I have need to be on fire, for I have mountains around me to melt."[9]

What makes a heart preacher? The heart preacher has some unusual spiritual qualities which are given to him only through the anointing of the Holy Spirit.

A heart preacher has a personal and intimate walk with God. A heart preacher has a compelling call to preach God's Word. He maintains the reality of his call through a rich devotional life.

A heart preacher loves his people. John Stott says, "Sometimes preachers use the pulpit to preach 'good chidings' rather than good tidings."[10] B. E. Morris, who died at the age of one hundred plus, was my mentor during the beginning days of my ministry in North Carolina. After he had served the great Greystone Baptist Church in Durham, North Carolina for twenty years, he retired. Shortly thereafter I asked him, "Brother Morris, if you had your ministry to do over, would you change anything?" Without hesitation, this strong, determined man replied, "Yes, Bill, I'd love people more."

A heart preacher is moved by the great truths of God's Word. If the preacher is moved, he can move others. If he has fire in his soul, he will put fire in others. A young preacher asked DeWitt Talmadge to critique his sermon after he heard him preach. So after the great preacher had listened to the message, he said to the young man, "Put some fire in your sermon, or put your sermon in the fire."

A preacher becomes a heart preacher when he has experienced heartbreak himself. God seems to use nothing until it is broken. George W. Truett became a heart preacher after the heartbreaking experience of accidentally shooting a close friend. Vance Havner became a greater preacher after the death of his wife, Sarah.[11] As the preacher looks out upon his people, he should remind himself that in every pew there is a broken heart.

Receiving the Anointing

How can a preacher receive this anointing, equipping him to preach in power and from the heart? The Bible does not give us successive steps to take in receiving the anointing. But the Bible does describe the kind of men God anoints, and history corroborates this description.

Anointed preachers are genuinely born again. John Wesley discovered after years of preaching that he had never experienced the message he was preaching. He then received the assurance of his own salvation and began to preach in the power of the Holy Spirit. Be sure of your own new birth. Jesus asked, "Can the blind lead the blind? Will they not both fall into the ditch?" (Luke 6:39).

Anointed preachers feel the burden of the Lord to proclaim His Word. This burden is produced by the Word and the Spirit, agape love, and the crushing needs of humankind.

Anointed preachers lead holy lives. Robert McCheyne said, "It is not great talents God blesses but great likeness to Jesus." "Be clean, you who bear the vessels of the LORD" (Isa. 52:11).

Anointed preachers live in brokenness and humility. Proud Simon Peter had to be broken before he preached with power. I believe he was giving his own personal testimony when he wrote 1 Peter 5:5, "Be clothed with humility, for God resists the proud, but gives grace to the humble."

The anointed preacher is an earnest student of the Bible. To be filled with the Spirit is to be filled with the Word. Ezra found power to speak to a backslidden people from the Word of God. He first studied the Word himself, then he put it into practice, and then he taught the Word to his people (see Ezra 7:10).

Anointed preachers are mighty in prayer. Robert McCheyne said, "A calm hour with God is worth a lifetime with men." No preacher can expect the anointing of the Spirit unless he spends much time alone with God. Pericles, the brilliant Athenian leader, said he deemed speaking so solemn an assignment that he never spoke without seeking the assistance of the immortal gods. And no preacher should approach the sacred pulpit until he has invoked the power of heaven upon his preaching.

Anointed preachers are set on pleasing God, not men. They are willing to be different. They are thermostats, regulating the spiritual temperature, rather than thermometers, registering it.

Anointed preachers learn to listen to God before speaking for God.[12] The spokesman for God must know more than the written word (the *logos*). He must pray and seek God until God impresses his heart with a specific but personal word *(rhema)* derived from the word in general *(logos)*.

Anointed preachers are ever seeking to be filled and refilled with the Holy Spirit. Jerry Vines makes an impassioned plea for the preacher to seek the anointing constantly:

> We must seek the Spirit's anointing. Ask Him to come on you and your message. Allow Him to manifest His power in and through you.

Never be satisfied with anything less in your sermon delivery. You may not always experience the power of the Holy Spirit upon your preaching in equal measure. For reasons in the realm of the mysterious, there are times when the anointing comes upon us in larger measure than at other times. . . . But there should be such surrender of life to the Spirit that every time we preach there is evidence of God's blessings upon us.[13]

When we speak of the anointing of the Holy Spirit, we are generally thinking of his aid in delivering the sermon. But not only is the Holy Spirit the divine Communicator, but he is also the divine Interpreter. Thus he helps us in preparing our sermons as well as in delivering them. The Holy Spirit enables the preacher to interpret Scripture correctly, discern its deeper meaning, quote it accurately, preach it clearly, and apply it incisively.

Moreover, the Holy Spirit can guide us in choosing the right Scripture passage for each occasion; He can guide us in books to purchase in the study of the Bible. He can give us illumination and insight in studying the passage. Dr. William Barclay calls the Holy Spirit "The Great Remembrancer," since he aids the believer's memory in recalling parallel passages and fitting illustrations. The Holy Spirit gives us joy and strength to push through the writing of the sermon.[14]

The anointing of the Holy Spirit is an absolute necessity for the preacher. I fervently appeal to every preacher to seek the Spirit's anointing constantly. I know no better way to do this than to quote the appeal of one of the most anointed preachers of the twentieth century, Martyn Loyd-Jones.

Seek this power, expect this power, yearn for this power; and when the power comes, yield to Him. Do not resist. Forget all about your sermon if necessary. Let Him loose you. Let Him manifest His power in you and through you. I am certain . . . that nothing but a return to this power of the Spirit on our preaching is going to avail us anything . . . it is the greatest need of all today. Seek it until you have it; be content with nothing less. Go on until you can say, "And my speech and my preaching was not with enticing words of man's wisdom, but in demonstration of the Spirit and of power." He is still able to do exceeding abundantly above all that we can ask or think.[15]

Conclusion

✳ Ten Commandments of Preaching

1. Preparing three messages each week is utterly and undeniably impossible without God's help.

2. Never preach about "my opinion" but always about God's revelation.

3. Seldom is a good sermon the result of instant inspiration; most often it comes from abundant perspiration.

4. Always speak with people, never to people.

5. A short, bad sermon is unforgivable. A long, bad sermon is unforgivable. A long, good sermon is forgettable (too much of a good thing is a bad thing). A short, good sermon is memorable (stand up, speak up, and shut up).

6. Be a pastor who cares enough to sit with those who are being hurt, and be a prophet who dares enough to stand against those who are hurting others.

7. Eyes right, left, center, and even an occasional about face to take in the choir.

8. Internalize the message to be relatively or completely free from notes and free to adapt if people's eyes start roving or closing. If you cannot remember the sermon, no one else will.

*By Paul R. Baxter, Pastor, First Baptist Church, La-Grange, Georgia.

9. Say absolutely nothing unless it can be said with great enthusiasm and expectation.
10. Follow the apostle Paul's example of relying not on oratorical or philosophical ability but simply on the gospel testimony about Jesus and Him crucified.

Notes

Part 1

Chapter 1—The Power of Preaching

1. Andrew W. Blackwood, *The Preparation of Sermons* (Nashville: Abingdon Press, 1948), 13.

2. W. E. Sangster, *The Craft of the Sermon* (London: Epworth, 1954), 7.

3. Martyn Loyd-Jones, *Preaching and Preachers* (Grand Rapids: Zondervan, 1972), 9, 297.

4. John R. Stott, *Between Two Worlds: The Art of Preaching in the Twentieth Century* (Grand Rapids: Wm. B. Eerdmans Publishing Co., 1982), 15.

5. Blackwood, *Preparation,* 13.

6. C. H. Dodd has established this fact in his *Apostolic Preaching and Its Development* (London: Hodder and Stoughton, 1936).

7. H. G. Brown, H. Gordon Clinard, and James J. Northcutt, *Steps to the Sermon* (Nashville: Broadman Press, 1963), 238.

8. Ibid., 29.

9. Quoted in Douglas M. White, *The Excellence of Exposition* (Neptune, NJ: Loizeaux Brothers, 1977), 16.

10. Ibid., 17.

11. Ibid., 18.

12. Ibid., 26.

13. Ibid., 31.

14. Ibid., 31.

15. Ibid., 32.

16. Ibid., 33–34.

17. Ibid., 35.

Chapter 2—But What Happened to the Power?

1. Stott, *Between Two Worlds,* 50.
2. G. Campbell Morgan, *Preaching* (Grand Rapids: Baker Book House, reprint 1971), 18.
3. Loyd-Jones, *Preaching*, 13.
4. Stott, *Between Two Worlds,* 84.
5. Ibid., 75.
6. Loyd-Jones, *Preaching,* 13.
7. Ibid., 17.
8. Ibid., 18.
9. Stott, *Between Two Worlds,* 89.

Part 2

Chapter 3—The Nature of Expository Preaching

1. Stott, *Between Two Words,* 126.
2. Faris D. Whitesell, *Power in Expository Preaching* (Old Tappan, NJ: Fleming H. Revell, 1963), f1—v11.
3. Ibid., xv.
4. Craig Skinner, "Palatable Expository Preaching," *Proclaim,* July-September 1979, 40.
5. Haddon Robinson, *Biblical Preaching* (Grand Rapids: Baker, 1980), 20.
6. Whitesell, *Power,* 17–30.
7. Ibid., 38.
8. Merrill F. Unger, *Principles of Expository Preaching* (Grand Rapids: Zondervan, 1955), 39–46.
9. Ibid., 48.
10. Ibid., 49
11. Ibid.
12. Ibid., 49–50.

13. Ibid., 51.

14. Ibid., 52.

15. Ibid., 52–53.

16. Robinson, *Biblical Preaching,* 57.

17. Stott, *Between Two Worlds,* 127–29.

Chapter 4—The Biblical Foundations of Expository Preaching

1. Stott, *Between Two Worlds,* 101.

2. Ibid., 102–3.

3. Ibid., 105.

4. Andrew W. Blackwood, *Preaching from the Bible* (New York: Abingdon, 1941), 182.

5. Unger, *Principles,* 18.

Chapter 5—The Nature of Evangelistic Preaching

1. V. L. Stanfield, *Effective Evangelistic Preaching* (Grand Rapids: Baker, 1965), 12–13.

2. Ibid., 15.

3. Ibid., 20.

Chapter 6—An Evaluation: Expository and Evangelistic Preaching

1. Jerry Vines, *A Practical Guide to Sermon Preparation* (Chicago: Moody, 1985), 64.

2. F. B. Meyer, *Expository Preaching* (Grand Rapids: Baker, 1974), 49–50.

3. Vines, *A Practical Guide,* 20.

4. Robinson, *Biblical Preaching,* 25.

5. White, *Excellence,* 40.

6. Ibid., 41.

7. Robinson, *Biblical Preaching,* 26.

8. Ibid., 27.

Part 3

Chapter 7—Armed in Spirit, Body, and Soul

1. Robinson, *Biblical Preaching*, 24.
2. Ibid., 28.
3. Haddon Robinson has an excellent section on "The Tools of the Trade" in his book *Biblical Preaching*, 60–65.

Chapter 8—Preparing Expository Sermons

1. Stott, *Between Two Worlds*, 48.
2. Vines, *Practical Guide*, xii.
3. Loyd-Jones, *Preaching*, 119.
4. Stott, *Between Two Worlds*, 214.
5. Morgan, *Preaching*, 50.
6. C. H. Spurgeon, "An All-Round Ministry," *Banner of Truth*, reprint 1960, 124.
7. Vines, *Practical Guide*, 8.
8. Stott, *Between Two Worlds*, 221–22.
9. Robinson, *Biblical Preaching*, 20–21.
10. Stott, *Between Two Worlds*, 229.
11. Ibid., 230.
12. William Tuck, "George Buttrick," *Proclaim*, October–December, 1985, 44.
13. Robinson, *Biblical Preaching*, 160.
14. Loyd-Jones, *Preaching*, 271ff.
15. Quoted in Warren Wiersbe, *Walking with the Giants* (Grand Rapids: Baker, 1976), 268.

Chapter 9—Preparing Evangelistic Sermons

1. Robert E. Coleman, *The Calling of an Evangelist*, ed. by J. D. Douglas, (Minneapolis: World Wide, 1987), 175–81.
2. Dr. Lewis Sperry Chafer, *True Evangelism* (Grand Rapids: Zondervan, 1919), 93.

3. Coleman, *Calling,* 77.

4. Ibid., 77.

5. Ibid., 177.

6. Ibid.

7. Quoted by Coleman, *Calling,* 178.

8. Ibid.

9. Quoted in R. A. Anderson, *The Shepherd-Evangelist* (Washington: Review and Herald, 1950), 190–91.

10. Ibid.

11. Coleman, *Calling,* 179.

12. Quoted in Coleman, *Calling,* 180.

13. Quoted in Coleman, *Calling,* 179.

14. Ibid., 180.

Chapter 10—Methods of Sermon Delivery

1. Vines, *Practical Guide,* 164.

2. Ibid., 165.

3. Andrew W. Blackwood, *Expository Preaching for Today* (Grand Rapids: Baker, 1943), 157.

Chapter 11—Some Dangers to Avoid

1. Loyd-Jones, *Preaching,* 264.

2. Ibid., 255.

3. Ibid., 256.

4. Ibid., 261.

5. Robinson, *Biblical Preaching,* 165.

Chapter 12—In the Power of the Spirit

1. Robinson, *Biblical Preaching,* 25.

2. Vines, *Practical Guide,* 157.

3. Loyd-Jones, *Preaching,* 307.

4. Vines, *Practical Guide*, 158.

5. Stott, *Between Two Worlds,* 334.

6. Billy Graham, *The Holy Spirit* (Waco: Word, 1978), 102.

7. Loyd-Jones, *Preaching,* 305.

8. Ibid., 324.

9. Vines, *Practical Guide,* 76.

10. Stott, *Between Two Worlds*, 212.

11. I am indebted to Jerry Vines for much of this material on the heart preacher: Vines, *Practical Guide*, 157.

12. Robinson, *Biblical Preaching,* 25.

13. Vines, *Practical Guide,* 162–63.

14. Whitesell, Power, 139–40.

15. Loyd-Jones, *Preaching,* 325.